A Pilgrimage of Hope:

A Story of Faith and Medicine

Mary McCarthy

authorHOUSE

AuthorHouse™
1663 Liberty Drive
Bloomington, IN 47403
www.authorhouse.com
Phone: 1 (800) 839-8640

Published by AuthorHouse 08/28/2015

ISBN: 978-1-5049-2627-0 (sc)
ISBN: 978-1-5049-2626-3 (e)

Library of Congress Control Number: 2015912100

Print information available on the last page.

Any people depicted in stock imagery provided by Thinkstock are models, and such images are being used for illustrative purposes only. Certain stock imagery © Thinkstock.

This book is printed on acid-free paper.

TABLE OF CONTENTS

ACKNOWLEDGEMENTS

I would like to thank Jim, my husband, for his never-ending support during my treatments and his love for me to this day.

My daughter, Kathleen, who gave me her comforting expression of love with physical therapy during my illness. She encouraged me to write this book.

My two sons, Tim and John and their spouses, Jane and Lindsay for their love sent from afar.

Additionally, I would like to thank my siblings, in-laws, family and friends for their encouragement and prayers.

I extend my gratitude to the CaringBridge readers who held me up in prayer when life challenged me the most. This book comes from the CaringBridge entries.

I thank Julie Rooke's edits to this book.

Finally, I would like to thank the members of the Rochester Public Library Critique Group, especially Mike Kalmbach, Amy Sullivan and Lois Kennis. I appreciate everyone who read and critiqued my submissions and believed in my mission to write this book.

INTRODUCTION

A pool of blood surrounded my head as I lay on the kitchen floor. My broken glasses and cell phone rested several feet away. Orienting myself to time and place allowed me to recall I was home and it was April 5, 2011.

"What happened?" I mused.

I assumed that I had fainted. I climbed the stairs to shower. Fainting didn't seem that big of a deal. After I cleaned myself up, I laundered the bloodied clothing.

Jim arrived home from the office later than usual that evening. The mask of fatigue he wore when he came through the door morphed quickly to shocked concern. As he saw my prizefighter face, he asked, "What happened to you?"

"I think I fainted today."

"I am taking you to the emergency room. I want you checked out," Jim replied in a low steady voice.

After taking a history, the medical staff examined me, and did a CT scan in the Emergency Room at Saint Marys Hospital. The doctors determined that I had experienced a seizure. They admitted me to the hospital so they could run more tests to show the cause.

Over the next 12 hours, I had an MRI, CT scan, EEG, and blood work. When I returned to my hospital room that afternoon, I found Jim sitting on the window ledge waiting for me. I settled into bed and Jim scooped me into his arms and cried, "Honey, you have brain cancer."

Those five words I heard on April 6, 2011, "Honey, you have brain cancer," may have altered my journey in life. They didn't alter my philosophy: Turn to the Lord with your troubles and have trust in God's plan. He will not abandon you.

I hope this book will inspire you no matter what challenges you face in your lifetime.

CHAPTER 1

Growing Up Catholic

I grew up in Prairie Village, Kansas, a suburb of Kansas City, the daughter of World War II veterans. My dad, John Beverly Cameron, enlisted in the Navy in 1940. Bev, as he was known, served on the Destroyer Escort USS *Frost* in the Atlantic. He served as Lt. Commander on the LST 1082 in the South Pacific. He retired as Commander in 1946 and returned to his home in Kansas City, Missouri.

My mom, Mary Monica Farrell, enlisted in the Army in 1943. As a college graduate with a degree in dietetics, Monica entered as a Second Lieutenant. The Army stationed her in Saipan in the South Pacific. At the end of the war, she enrolled at St. Louis University to earn her Master's Degree in Dietetics.

I am the second of seven children, four boys and three girls. My parents were devout Catholics and my primary role models. They planted a seed of faith and kept it moist to develop deep roots. I followed the Catholic traditions by taking part in the sacraments, going to Mass, and serving others by living the Beatitudes. As adults, my siblings and I are prayer warriors for each other when we encounter problems in our lives.

I attended Catholic grade school and high school. I learned the Catechism through memorization from the Baltimore edition under the watchful eyes of the Sisters of Mercy. As students, we didn't talk about ideas beyond the literal meaning of the printed word. I recited the answers: "Why did God make you?"

"To know Him, love Him, and serve Him in this world and be happy with Him in heaven."

I said my prayers as part of the Catholic ritual and Catholic guilt. I feared sin and disgrace. Practicing my religion became habit forming.

After I graduated from the University of Kansas with a degree in Business Administration, I married a wonderful Catholic man. Jim and I moved to Rochester, Minnesota so he could do his residency in Internal Medicine at Mayo Clinic. We are now in our 35th year of that plan! Rochester was a good place to raise our family of two sons and a daughter.

Because my spouse and I both had a Catholic education, we sent our three children to Catholic schools in Rochester. These institutions did a great job of preparing students both academically and spiritually. Our commitment to the Church as adults was kept alive by participating with our children in the sacraments, liturgy, and in service to others. I continued to sprinkle the seed of faith that my parents had sowed. My convictions blossomed as I shared them with my family.

It was time to harvest my spiritual garden when my nest dwindled to empty as I sent each child off to college. My beliefs ran on autopilot, but my thirst for more enrichment became stronger. I explored adult faith formation programs through our parish.

The enhancements to my faith began in a subtle way. In 2001, I began to spend Sunday nights in quiet reflection with God through Eucharistic Adoration. I came to treasure that hour of private prayer in front of the Body of Christ in the chapel of our church.

I bought a study Bible so I could read God's word each week at Adoration. Reading the Bible as a novel didn't work, so I joined a Bible Study at our church led by Jeff Cavins. The name of the course was *The Great Adventure: A Journey Though the Bible.* His teaching of the Bible peeled back the layers of memorized Catechism. I started to understand the history and the message of the Bible. I thirsted for the knowledge of my religion and sought religious books and CDs on Catholicism and the Bible. Jim and I added a pilgrimage to the Holy Land with Mr. Cavins when the opportunity and budget allowed.

In reflecting on where I am today, I am aware God has a path for me, but he hasn't shared it with me. I am amazed by God's unconditional love for me and I profoundly appreciate these themes: Silence, Listening, Trust, Challenge, Action, Thanksgiving, Family, Relationships, Wonder, and Awe. I continue to fertilize the kernel of faith on a journey to do His will. He has a plan for me.

CHAPTER 2

Meet the McCarthys

Jim and I became proud parents when I gave birth to our first son, Tim, in 1978. He grew into a mild-mannered youth. He focused on details in his creative Lego designs, crafting a gingerbread house with exquisite candy décor, or sculpting his winning Pinewood Derby car. Tim excelled in school, dribbled the basketball, played saxophone in the band, and was an Eagle Scout. It did not surprise us when he earned a Master's degree in Architecture. He moved to London in 2002 to start his career as an architect. While he was working in London, he met his bride, Jane, a radiographer, who worked at Lister Hospital in Chelsea.

In 2006, Jane married Tim in Hamilton, New Zealand, where Jane's family lives. The story of their courtship and marriage rivaled that of a best-selling novel. They encountered miles of red tape as they tried to get Jane's Green Card. This international couple wanted to move to the U.S. On the other hand, Tim had no trouble when he applied for and received British citizenship.

In 2010, when Jane was ready to deliver their first child, Emma, it opened their eyes to the National Health System in London. It was nothing like in the U.S. Tim and Jane had to pre-schedule a taxi to take them to the hospital, provide their own food and towels, as well as everything for the baby, including diapers! After Jane delivered her precious baby girl, she was in a ward with six other women.

Tim and Jane called us on Christmas 2010, to say the Permanent Green Card application was in order. Jane could enter the country and Tim could transfer his job from London to New York. This news delighted us!

They arrived at JFK during one of the worst blizzards in history. Old Man Winter did not concern them since this move had been their focus for nearly five years. We flew to New York to visit them in March 2011. They had a spacious apartment in a quaint village north of Manhattan. Jane was taking driving classes, and she did a good job of giving us a ride on the "correct" side of the road.

***

In 1980, we welcomed the birth of our second son, John, to our family. He brought a lively spirit to our household. John was athletic, and he tried a variety of sports: hockey, basketball and baseball. He was a guy-on-the-go with an engaging personality. John played trumpet in band and was an Eagle Scout. He studied Economics in college and later he merited an MBA. While in college, John met his wife, Lindsay, also an Economics major.

John married Lindsay in 2005, in Minneapolis. John works in real estate financing. Lindsay works three days a week at a job at General Mills. When they started a family, I had the honor of driving one hundred miles each way on Mondays to be a Granny Nanny. Reagan was our first granddaughter, born in 2007 and Dylan followed twenty months later. I held that position from January 2008-December 2010. Commutes during the Minnesota winters were a challenge, but like the old post office motto, "The mail must go through" so too, "the granny must go through." A deer encounter late one night on the drive home didn't dampen my commitment.

While engaged with granny care in the nice weather, the grandchildren were happy to ride their bikes or draw with chalk on their driveway. Summer outings included walks to nearby parks, or even to the Pet Smart in a strip mall to view the animals in their cages. When it was naptime, I would say, "It is prayer time." I wanted them to develop a faith foundation. I napped when they napped in the afternoon so I could be alert for the drive back to Rochester.

The two-hour commute up and back gave me time to listen to CD classes. I developed an appreciation for the religion courses offered by The Teaching Company (check out www.thegreatcourses.com). I also listened to Bible Study CDs taught by Jeff Cavins.

***

In 1988, God blessed us with our daughter, Kathleen. She was the second girl born to the McCarthy clan over the last five generations. Her two older brothers spoiled her. They entertained her by reading books and gifting her with enthusiasm for life. Whenever Tim or John had a scouting, music or sporting event, Kathleen attended. Girl Scouts kept her active, and she liked to camp. In high school, she played trumpet and baritone in the band and chased tennis balls around the court. In addition, Kathleen developed a love for Latin due to her teacher's passion for this classical field. Her affinity for the classics started when she was just ten-years-old when our family traveled to Rome: she soaked in the Roman history, culture, and architecture.

Kathleen attends the University of Wisconsin at Madison. She will graduate with degrees in both Classical Languages (emphasis in Greek and Latin) and Classical Humanities. When asked what a person with a degree in the Classics does for a job or profession, Kathleen admits that she does not have a clear vision of her career. However, she is an academic girl with a Ph.D. in her future.

***

I retired from my Granny Nanny position in January 2011. Volunteerism had been something I had taken to heart during the years of raising our three children, so I changed my center of attention for Mondays. I worked to create a new program for the recently formed St. Vincent de Paul (SVDP) conference at our parish, the Church of the Resurrection. The "Helping Hands" ministry would be a voucher for a meal and bus tickets to be distributed to less fortunate members throughout the community. I applied for a $5000 grant from the Knights of Columbus, and was awarded the funds on April 1, 2011. The Helping Hands ministry became a reality in the SVdP Society in each Catholic parish in Rochester.

There are many other things I enjoy doing in my free time. I delight in my perennial garden outside my front door. It is like seeing old friends when they emerge from the ground after a cold snowy winter.

I make it a point to go to the gym three days a week. It is a social outing as much as exercise. My endorphins are noticeably higher on the days I exercise.

I had the opportunity to work part-time at the local Herberger's department store, where I am legendary for sniffing out the best deals. I could go broke saving us money. Jim jokes that my tombstone will read, "This, too, was on sale."

***

Jim is a dedicated husband, father, and grandfather. He has brought joy, laughter and wisdom to our 36 years of marriage. Jim is the Chair of the Division of Nephrology (kidney) and Hypertension at Mayo Clinic. He is challenged by the ever-changing health care system in the U.S. Playing golf has been an obsession with Jim since the days of his youth. Jim has a single digit handicap. Genealogy and wine-making are just two of his other hobbies.

We both love to travel despite the security hassles and airline schedules. When I put together the reservations, I go into "Mary Mode." I should have been a travel agent. Our favorite vacations have been on sailboats in the Caribbean or South Pacific. Jim pursued his dream of scuba diving on the Great Barrier Reef, while I preferred to snorkel. It has been fun for us to experience the diversity of cultures, geography, food, and climates around the world.

Most of our family remains in Kansas City, so we often call on friends in Rochester to share the joys and trials of life. We are blessed to have the richness of friends woven in our lives.

CHAPTER 3

Journal Entries
Emergency Room and Diagnosis

April 5, 2011

On my way to work today, I began my holy quest. I mailed a deposit for our January, 2012 pilgrimage to the Holy Land. Jeff Cavins, a Bible scholar from Minnesota, would lead the group. Jim and I had been taking Jeff's classes for several years and desired to expand our knowledge of the Bible by traveling to the sites where the gospels had taken place. The timing and funding for this trip had come to maturity. I had no inkling the pilgrimage would have a detour before we would leave.

After I finished working an early shift at the department store, I came home to eat lunch at the kitchen table. Jim and I were flying to Vancouver the next day so Jim could attend a nephrology (kidney) conference. I crossed things off my "to do" list as I ate; it appeared the only tasks left to finish were the laundry and packing. After I finished lunch, I cleared my plate and glass to the sink.

The next thing I remember was waking up in a pool of blood on the kitchen floor. I sat up and pulled myself up to a kitchen chair. As the fog in my head eased, I remembered that I was getting ready to pack.

I made my way to the near-by bathroom and looked in the mirror. My face resembled the face of a boxer with black eyes, a broken nose, and misplaced teeth. What had happened to me? I must have been in shock as I shrugged off the spell.

I thought I must have fainted. Fainting didn't seem like a big deal. Warning bells should have gone off in my mind. I realize that now. It never occurred to me that something might be dreadfully wrong. I downplay medical emergencies as evidenced in an event in 1991.

***

On Halloween, 1991, a snowstorm approached southeast Minnesota. Jim had tickets for himself and our two sons, ages ten and twelve, to attend the Chicago Bulls basketball game on Friday, November 1st. They also had tickets to the Notre Dame football game in South Bend, Indiana, on Saturday, November 2nd. Jim, Tim, and John left early for the road trip to Chicago on November 1st because they needed to get ahead of the storm.

I stayed home with our three-year-old daughter, Kathleen. She and I intended to go to a juvenile concert in Rochester on Friday night, but the blowing snow led to its cancelation. We were sorry that the concert had to be canceled, but remained upbeat with the inches of winter wonderland that were accumulating. The chance to go sledding this early in the season made Kathleen happy.

Jim called after the basketball game to say the Bulls had won. Tim and John saw Michael Jordan, the star of the Chicago Bulls, play a good game. The boys were excited to head to South Bend the next morning.

When I got up on Saturday morning, I wasn't feeling well. I had nausea and cramps. I gave Kathleen permission to climb on the counter to fill her bowl with Cheerios for breakfast. (In retrospect, I can't imagine encouraging a three-year-old to reach for a dish and cereal.) The dog needed to go out, so I crawled to the door to let him out. My mom called from Kansas City to inquire about our record snowfall of twenty-two inches. I said I had the flu. I rested on the sofa while Kathleen played and watched way too much TV. We went to bed early on Saturday night.

Jim and the boys joined the crowded stadium of fans at the Notre Dame game to see the Fighting Irish win their game. They drove back to Chicago to spend the night before returning home on Sunday.

On Sunday morning, I could hardly stand. I crawled down the stairs in military fashion and paged through Jim's medical books. I considered my symptoms and wondered if I had an ectopic pregnancy. The description correlated to what I was experiencing.

I called Jim before he started his drive home from Chicago. I told him how I felt. He asked me to call our good friends, and neighbors, Kathy and Tom, and ask them to take me to the Emergency Room at Saint Marys Hospital.

Immediately after talking to me, Jim called Kathy and Tom and told them I had a ruptured appendix. Later, we learned how accurate his phone diagnosis had been. Kathy drove over to pick me up. She recognized I was sick when I opened the door wearing my glasses, not my contacts, and a robe over my nightgown. It shocked Kathy to see the ransacked house. Kathleen played with anything she wanted and did not have to put her toys away. Kathy dropped Kathleen off at their home to play with her daughter and husband and whisked me to Saint Marys Hospital.

I recalled answering a litany of questions in the ER about my health history and medications. They took x-rays. The staff poked my abdomen as if I was the Pillsbury Dough Boy. Our cardiologist friend, André, showed up in the ER as a substitute in Jim's role since he realized Jim was driving home from Chicago. I overheard the staff when they said that they intended to insert a subclavian catheter. I shrieked. "I do not want that."

André calmly stated, "This is what Jim would want."

I had heard the term for this catheter before and I understood it was larger and used to allow fluids to be delivered faster. I didn't realize how sick I was.

After confirming that I had a ruptured appendix and was septic, they took me to surgery. Sepsis is a life-threatening infection in the blood stream caused by toxin-producing bacteria.

Jim arrived at the hospital as the orderly wheeled me out of the operating room. I lived on a respirator in the Intensive Care Unit for several days. When I improved, they moved me to a regular room for a week of nursing care. I have little memory of either my ICU or hospital stay. I recalled Jim brought our children to the hospital to visit me. He wanted the kids to see that sick people recover. Optimism is Jim's middle name. Kathleen brought her Fisher-Price doctor kit to check me over.

Flowers filled my room to where I wondered if I had died. Later, I learned the many wonderful acts of kindness extended to my family and me: concerned inquiries, countless prayers, as well as rides for my kids and meals for us all. I appreciated the people in my life and said a prayer of thanksgiving to God. I was grateful He had brought me through this medical crisis. *Trust in God* became my mantra.

My son, Tim, had an English assignment soon after my illness and he wrote the following poem. I keep this in my jewelry box with items precious to me.

Aromas of sweet-smelling roses, petunias,
and peonies

Chrysanthemums and begonias, galore.

Some marigold and honeysuckle and azaleas

Enough to fill a botanical garden!

My mother slept-

With a mask on her mouth, and needles in her arms,

She clung to life through an artificial respirator.

Watching through the clouds in my eyes,

The longing for a healthy mother overwhelmed me.

Desiring a return to standard – day happenings

I turned and asked, "Why God? Why MY mom?"

***

Twenty years later, I dismissed this emergency as a fainting spell. Maybe I was in denial that something was seriously wrong. I climbed the stairs to shower. I added the bloodied clothing to the laundry.

Jim looked exhausted by the time he got home from work. He took one look at my prizefighter face. With the obvious sound of concern in his voice he asked, "What happened to you?" I couldn't imagine the possible scenarios going on in his mind.

"I think I fainted today," I said calmly.

"I am taking you to the Emergency Room."

"Why do I have to go to the ER for fainting?" I asked.

"I want you checked out." I've learned to listen to him when he talks in a professional tone. Deep down, I too wanted to know why I had fainted.

"What tests will they do?"

"Routine exam, check your vital signs and ask about your medications."

"Do you think we will need to change our plane reservations for tomorrow?"

"That is a decision we will make later," Jim replied in a confident voice.

On the drive to the hospital, we chatted about our Vancouver trip. "I can't wait to check-in at the hotel with the gas fireplace in the room." We had a slate of places to shop and see when Jim wasn't in meetings.

"I would like to go on a harbor cruise," Jim said, "and visit the Van Duson Botanical Gardens." We expected to see flowers in bloom.

"I am bringing my Merrells to hike on Grouse Mountain."

Jim had searched the Internet for seafood restaurants we might try near the waterfront as we enjoy the cuisine of a new city when we travel.

When we arrived in the Emergency Room at Saint Marys Hospital, the nurses and resident physicians began their evaluation. They drilled me with questions of my symptoms that brought me to the hospital. The physical appearance of my face was a good clue. I informed them of my health history and medications.

"I am healthy. I work out at Dan Abraham Healthy Living Center (a Mayo sponsored facility); eat right, including chocolate; drink wine occasionally; and my medications are a daily vitamin, a calcium pill, and Premarin."

The ER staff did a physical exam and took my vital signs. Through Houdini magic, they changed me into a flimsy hospital gown that offered no modesty. I focused on the trip to Vancouver.

I sat on a bed in the ER. After the basic exam, the doctors did a neurological exam. This comprised several parts. "Can you tell us the name of the President?"

"Obama," I replied.

"Do you know where you are right now?"

"I am in Saint Marys Emergency Room."

"Do you know today's date?"

"April 5th."

I passed the mental status evaluation.

The doctors tested my optic nerve using a flashlight. "Follow the light with your eyes without moving your head."

The motor exam determined muscle strength. "Can you raise your arms and bend them at your elbow while I press down on your arms?" the doctor asked. I obeyed.

"Let me see you raise your leg at the knee while I press down on it." Again, I complied. Why were they doing these tests I wondered?

"I want to see you tap your pointer finger and thumb." I had minimal trouble with this request.

The reflex test was straightforward with the doctor tapping my elbow and knee with his hammer. My reflexes were great.

"Can you use your pointer finger to touch my finger and then your nose?" I did as they asked.

"I need you to walk heel-to-toe in a straight line." Was this a sobriety test? I was grateful for the time and tests, but wanted to get home so I would be rested for the flight to Vancouver the next day.

Doctors used pins and tongue depressors to measure my sense of touch. So far, I figured I'd sailed through these unnecessary tests with little concern.

I had a computerized tomography (CT) scan of my head. A CT scan is an imaging study that uses x-rays to produce images of the internal parts of the body, in this case, the brain. I lay on a movable table and technicians slid me into a donut-shaped machine. The machine rotated around and took pictures that the radiologists used to interpret and diagnose my condition. It impressed me that they were giving me such a thorough exam, although I didn't know what they were looking for. I assumed it would help explain why I fainted today.

When the test results came back, doctors determined I had experienced a seizure. A seizure is an uncontrolled spasm or convulsion caused by abnormal electrical activity in the brain. I learned my brain had electricity in it! Since I didn't have a history of seizures, they admitted me overnight to the hospital. They added other tests the next day. Sadly, a hospital stay replaced the trip to Vancouver. Jim said, "We can always go another time." He is a positive guy. We said our good nights, kissed, and Jim left the hospital.

April 6, 2011

Jim returned early before the neurologist made his rounds. The staff physician arrived, accompanied by residents, interns and nurses who asked me when the symptoms started and I gave them the information as best as I recalled. Over the next six hours, I had another CT scan, more blood work, an EEG, and a Magnetic Resonance Image (MRI) exam. I was a frequent flier in the MRI machine as I had this test before two back surgeries. I did not understand, or ask, what today's tests were for, remaining positive that there was nothing seriously wrong.

When I came back to my hospital room on a gurney after the morning tests, Jim waited for me. After I settled into bed, Jim climbed in next to me, scooped me into his arms and cried.

"Honey, you have brain cancer."

My first response was, "**NO!**"

We hugged each other and sobbed. We could not accept the diagnosis. We prayed. We asked why and how. I had no symptoms or headaches. I exercised and had eaten right so how was it possible I could have cancer? I thought my body had betrayed me. This disease strikes other people—not me!

I feared what the diagnosis meant. Was it fatal? How long did I have? What about the pilgrimage to the Holy Land? I had just mailed in our registration the previous day. Even Jim, an experienced physician, did not know where to turn next.

The neurosurgeon, Dr. Ian Parney, came to my hospital room to interpret the results. I heard Dr. Parney say the medical jargon, but I didn't understand the words. Jim entered "doctor" mode; I knew he would translate for me. Jim would have to explain it many times because, frankly, I was in shock.

Dr. Parney said, "I have looked at your MRI, Mary. It appears you have a brain tumor. You have two options: I can offer you surgery to remove the tumor or do a biopsy. There is lower risk with the biopsy. We can give a name and grade to the tumor with a biopsy. Because of where the tumor is located, there is greater risk if we do surgery. You might be paralyzed or not be able to talk."

It was a no-brainer (ha-ha!) for me. "Go for the biopsy," I said. That afternoon, the doctor discharged me from the hospital until a surgical biopsy date could be scheduled.

Because we had planned on being in Vancouver, we informed our three grown children that our cell phones would not work in Canada. We would communicate via e-mail. We knew we had to call each of them with this shocking news. We put the phone on speaker so both Jim and I could talk. Their surprise at getting a phone call from us turned to shock as we told them why we were still in Rochester. There was obvious concern for me as they each planned to come home at once. We asked them to wait and come for the biopsy. We called our extended families and dearest friends to tell them about the diagnosis. I cannot recall any of the conversations with my children, family, or friends. My life became a blur. I could not focus on the moment or the future as I was not in control. I felt like I had fallen into a deep abyss.

April 9-10, 2011

Our daughter, Kathleen, was alone in Madison at college, so Jim thought we should drive over and visit her for the weekend. We sought to reassure her that things would be all right. Were we trying to convince ourselves that life would go back to normal?

We reached Madison in record time and the three of us Skyped with her brothers, Tim and John. Jim hoped to set everyone's minds at rest that I would be fine. We had to stay hopeful and prayerful in this crisis.

Jim, Kathleen and I went to Saturday afternoon Mass, and the sermon was "Why do bad things happen to good people?" The answer was, "That is how God tests the good ones." Was I being challenged to be a witness to Christ in my life? I prayed to do His will.

After Mass, we ate dinner at our favorite restaurant and it satisfied the hunger of both body and spirit. We invited Kathleen to spend the night with us at our hotel.

I hated to leave Kathleen alone at school on Sunday morning. We promised she could come home for the biopsy. It was hard to accept the cancer diagnosis lingering in the air at all times.

April 11, 2011

Jim drove me to Apache Mall, where I worked at Herberger's department store. I went upstairs to the office to tell the store manager, Sharon, about my diagnosis. She cradled me in her arms.

Soon, the rest of the managers came into the office where I shared the diagnosis. Everyone was in tears. The assistant store manager called my friend and colleague, Susan, to the office so I could tell her the news myself. Sharon gave me a leave of absence since I didn't know when I might return to work.

Later that day, our sons and their families arrived in Rochester. Tim, Jane, and their eighteen-month-old daughter, Emma, flew to Rochester from New York. John, Lindsay, and their toddlers, Reagan and Dylan, drove down from Minneapolis. The house swelled with generations of family.

It became the story of the City Mouse and the Country Mouse with our grandchildren. Emma lives 30 minutes north of Manhattan, so she often accompanied her parents or visitors into New York City; she had an eager smile and played quietly. Reagan and Dylan entered the house, and they were noisy, loud, and fun. They lived in suburbia with access to lots of activities.

The cousins rarely got together. There was a bit of posturing who would be the pack leader. Reagan, age three, took the role. The two remaining grandkids fell in line. They adapted to a happy rhythm. The spring weather lured the kids to play on our cul-de-sac. We had kept the tricycles, chalk and balls in our arsenal of grandkid toys. Several neighbors welcomed them to climb and play on their swing sets. The children had joyous fun while the dark cloud of the diagnosis hung over the adults' heads.

April 12, 2011

My daughters-in-law drove to Madison to bring Kathleen home for the biopsy. For three days, we enjoyed having the family together under our roof. In the past, I would have spent delightful time in preparing for a family gathering. I would have arranged fun outings, planned menus, and baked yummy treats before their arrival. This time, the horror of cancer distracted me. Cancer stole my control as a hostess. I turned my kitchen over to Kathleen, Jane and Lindsay. Tim and John took over the supervision of their children while they played.

Each one of us spent those days together not knowing what to expect in the coming week and the near future. The surgical biopsy, scheduled for April 15, would give us more information and help determine the type and grade of tumor.

From the recent tests, we knew the location of the tumor, deep in the brain on the front left side in the temporal lobe. It was near the centers for speech and control of the right arm and leg. Because of this, it could not be removed safely without permanently damaging these areas. The doctors suspected one of two types of tumors—an oligodendroglioma or an astrocytoma—but it would take up to three days to get the final results.

News of my diagnosis spread like wildfire. People brought meals, cards, and gifts to our home. These kindnesses overwhelmed us. Love and prayers supported us. Kathleen started a list for thank you notes of meals and acts of kindness that friends and neighbors arranged for our family. She had a hard time keeping the list up-to-date.

Lindsay set up a CaringBridge site to keep family and friends informed with my medical status. We sent out a thank you from my CaringBridge for each thoughtful gesture.

The family room mantle and bookshelves became a display case for the many cards I received. One friend, Kathy, mailed me a card every day. A variety of the cards were humorous or spiritual. There was one card that said, "Manicures and Pedicures…I wish all Cures were that easy." I found comfort in the spiritual cards I received. Many people wrote Bible verses in the cards, which inspired me to fight this battle. The prayers of others provided me with strength to carry on in the face of my challenge. I placed myself in God's loving hands and asked Him to give me the gift of wisdom. I desired to be open to His will in the outcome of the biopsy. I whispered I would go where He leads me.

April 14, 2011

After the three grandchildren were in bed, we ate a delicious meal prepared by a neighbor. We held a family meeting. Jim interpreted the medical language so we could understand what would happen during the next day's biopsy in lay people's terms. We hugged each other, cried, and prayed the rosary together. The scene appeared surreal; it was one of those horror stories that happened to someone else.

April 15, 2011

We were up early today in order for us to be at Saint Marys Hospital by 5:30 a.m. Tim, John and Kathleen joined Jim and me, while Lindsay and Jane remained at home with the three children.

After I registered, a nurse directed me to a small room where I changed into a thin blue hospital gown. The nurse recorded my vital signs and medical information. The tiny room filled with those closest to me: Jim, my rock; our three children; a few close friends; and Father David Byrne. Fr. David led a prayerful chant before surgery. I cried with fear of the unknown.

When everyone left the pre-op cubicle, I lay on the gurney in the hallway waiting to be taken into the O.R. for surgery. I reflected on my mother and her battle with lung cancer in 2006. When Kathleen had asked my mom if she was afraid to die, she gave a little laugh and said, "Oh, no, honey. I have prepared for this my entire life."

My parents' strong faith as devout Catholics solidified my quest for eternal life. I felt drawn to my mom at this time and, in truth, I wanted to join her in heaven. The hope of a blessed reunion afforded me peace as they wheeled me into the operating room at 7 a.m.

Later, Jim told me it took Dr. Parney and his team three hours to do the scans necessary to decide the area to biopsy. The biopsy itself took seventy-five minutes. The post-biopsy scans showed no major bleeding, so they wheeled me to recovery. I was too groggy from the anesthesia to be tested for any effects on my speech or use of my right arm or leg. The preliminary results showed that the brain cancer was probably a "glioma." We would get the final results following week.

I arrived in the Neurosurgery Intensive Care Unit at 4 p.m., with a small patch above my left temple. This covered the two-inch incision held together by several staples. Luckily, my thick hair made the staples hard to see. I had a little weakness in the right arm and leg, but it was too early to know if I would have further complications. I had no pain, and was thirsty. As the evening wore on, drowsiness cleared, thanks to intravenous steroids given to reduce brain swelling. Carrot cake for dinner satisfied my giant sweet tooth. After all, carrot cake included the carrots as a vegetable and the cream cheese icing as a dairy exchange. I commandeered my iPhone to read the CaringBridge guest book entries.

April 16, 2011

Savoring carrot cake again for breakfast on Saturday was an indulgence. I applied my signature shade of lipstick, L'Oreal Sea Fleur, and watched the Weather Channel. These were signs of recovery and downright normalcy. My right arm and leg strength had improved significantly. I walked around the nurses' station without help, and I confidently moved around my room. The nurse removed my surgical bandage and the tiny incision was unobtrusive.

Dr. Parney came to my room to evaluate the next step in the treatment for my cancer. He is a kind and gentle physician and explained the surgery factually with tinges of optimism. "As the scans showed before surgery, we know where the tumor is located. It is near the speech and the control centers of your right arm and leg. I believe we were successful in getting the tissue needed for identifying the type and grade of tumor."

"When will the biopsy results be back?" I inquired.

"In about three days. Then we will plan a therapy for you. It will most likely involve radiation and chemotherapy. The possible complications could be swelling of the brain from the surgery or bleeding. If you experience anything significant, call us."

I remember everything happening so fast; the seizure, the diagnosis, the biopsy, and now I faced therapies to treat the cancer. I hoped I wouldn't experience anything significant when I went home.

A nurse set up an appointment to have the biopsy staples removed the next week. The doctor discharged me one day after the biopsy.

Jim made plans to cut his work schedule to eighty percent, working four days a week. He filled out the forms for the Family Medical Leave Act because he was spending extra time at the hospital with me. We did not know how much more time would be needed when I began the next phase of treatment.

At home, the CaringBridge site offered an amazing source of comfort and support for us. Jim didn't have to come home and call our family and friends to give them an update. Either Jim or I posted a daily update on the CaringBridge site about my medical care. I enjoyed reading the guest book entries as they encouraged me to keep hope in my field of vision. How incredible to have prayers and good wishes flowing twenty-four hours a day, seven days a week, from around the globe. I persevered by deepening my relationship with the Lord. I relied on His care. He is the Great Physician.

CHAPTER 4

The Good, the Bad and the Ugly

April 16, 2011

I arrived home from the hospital the day after the biopsy to a busy house filled with grandchildren. The kitchen overflowed with food, gifts, flowers, and get-well cards. The hospital sent me home with an aqua blue emesis bowl, Kleenex, an eyeglasses case, a small bottle of lotion, a toothbrush and an envelope with dismissal instructions. Clutter annoyed me. The untidiness from my discharge added to the chaos in my life.

Anxiety flourished while I waited for the biopsy results. I required a seat belt for this roller coaster of emotions until I found out what the biopsy results showed. A monster of doubt lurked in my head. How serious might my diagnosis be? Fear gripped me to the core.

At home, Kathleen escorted me to the family room where I saw and observed the three grandchildren at play. They entertained themselves with toys that I had saved from our three children. Reagan, who was three, loved the Fisher-Price doll house with its "Little People." Dylan, 18 months, preferred the toy trucks he discovered in the large Tupperware toy box. Emma, also 18 months, lined up small bears in a row. She reminded me of her dad, Tim, when he was a child. I leaned over on the sofa and left the lively scene before my eyes and fell asleep.

The children ate an early supper. Dylan's food allergies made meals difficult, and his mother, Lindsay, found it easier to have them eat first. Dinner precedes bath and bedtime in both households, so that ritual followed at grandma's house.

The adults waited until the grandchildren were in bed to dine together with barbeque food. We served the buffet-style feast on the kitchen counter. The gloomy faces from two nights ago gave way to laughter. We didn't expect any complications from the biopsy. We relayed old family stories to entertain Jane and Lindsay. Many tales revolved around our pet beagle, Lightning. We had to repeat the well-known tale about the way we came to acquire a dog.

***

When John was seven years old, he asked for a dog. As many mothers do, I tried to stall him. I said, "In the spring."

On Groundhog Day, John bounded down the stairs and shouted, "Goody! Six weeks from today, we get our dog! You said, 'In the spring.'" He must have heard on the radio it would be an early spring.

Our family scouted dog shows to consider what breed of dog we wanted, checked out library books, and researched how to train a dog. Tim and John decided on a beagle because of the size and temperament. I watched the newspaper for ads by a local breeder. We adopted Lightning on Mother's Day, 1988. He instantly became a member of the family. We established which areas of the house were out of bounds to Lightning. Everybody broke the rules. He brought joy to our household until his death in 2002.

***

Jim and I hugged and kissed our grown kids and spouses around 10 p.m. before we headed upstairs to bed. As we reached the bottom of the stairs, I heard the caps fly off the beer bottles as our adult children and their spouses toasted the successful surgery. I grinned as I held the handrail. It comforted me to be surrounded by a loving family.

After I brushed my teeth, donned a nightgown, and climbed into bed, I had a seizure. Jim yelled, "Call 911!" Kathleen got flustered when she placed the 911 call, so Lindsay grabbed the phone and gave the paramedics our address. Jane rushed upstairs. She and Jim watched me until the ambulance arrived. Tim called our friends, Ann and André, and asked them to meet us in the E.R. John called our neighbors, Kathy and Tom. I rested on the bed, confused and scared. Jim never took his eyes off me.

Our friend, Kathy, volunteered to stay with the sleeping children. Later, Kathleen told me, despite the commotion, the grandkids had stayed asleep.

The paramedics used a special chair to carry me down the stairs. They transferred me onto a gurney at the front door. The gurney was a bed on wheels that slid into the ambulance. Jim scrambled into the ambulance with me and one paramedic. Jim held my hand as we made our way back to the hospital. They didn't use their sirens nor did they drive fast because it wasn't a life-threatening situation. I shivered on the cold, bumpy ride.

Our children and spouses drove to Saint Marys Hospital. The biopsy party had been aborted.

A new CT scan in the E.R. showed no change from the post-op scan, but at 1 a.m., they admitted me to the ICU for observation.

"I want to go to Palm Sunday Mass tomorrow," I pleaded.

Jim spoke with a voice of authority, "You are excused from that obligation."

The doctors adjusted my drugs to help me get a good night's sleep. Since my diagnosis, Jim had spent most of his time with me, and tonight he rested on a cot in my room. Due to the drugs I was getting, I never knew if Jim was in the room with me. I didn't know the name of the enemy I fought in this cancer battle, but I knew God was orchestrating my care through the trained medical staff.

April 17, 2011

I had another seizure in the ICU today. The doctors ordered more tests and scans. They noted no change. Though I don't remember this, my nurse reported that I raised my right arm above my head and my eyes looked up to the right. I could talk, but I repeated things instead of answering the question. "Mary, can you put your arm down?" I would reply, "Mary, can you put your arm down?" They dispensed more anti-seizure medicine, and I slipped into a deep slumber.

My neuro-oncologist, Dr. Julie Hammack, was overseeing my care with each hospitalization. She checked in with the oncology team and my husband, as her busy schedule often took her out of town. Dr. Hammock dispensed orders through every type of media: phone, email, and text. I didn't realize the critical role she had in my medical care.

When I awoke, I could not move my right arm or leg. I could hold them up if someone moved them. That meant my physical strength was good, but my brain had a problem processing or coordinating the movement commands I gave. This was a terrifying experience. What if my right side remained paralyzed? By evening, this had improved. I asked God for the spiritual strength to recover.

The attentive nurses answered many of my questions about my diagnosis and what to expect on the road back to health. Lori, a thoughtful nurse, brought me a Caribou yogurt parfait. The smooth, cool texture of the yogurt refreshed and nourished me.

My neurosurgeon, Dr. Parney, and his chief resident, Dr. Daniels, made their hospital rounds. "We feel the trauma of the biopsy has caused the seizures." They had discussed this after the biopsy the day before, but I did not comprehend it in my foggy, post-operative state.

After John and his family attended Palm Sunday Mass at Saint Marys Hospital, they walked the long corridors to my hospital room. They gave me hugs and kisses before driving home to Minneapolis. It had meant the world to us to have them here.

With the Minnesota family gone, our close friends, André and Ann, Tom and Kathy, whom we pressed into service after the 911 call, came to visit me in the hospital. They kept me in good spirits. They joked with me about the frequent hospitalizations and my need for attention. My friend, Allison, brought a pair of bright pink bunny slippers that became my trademark in the hospital.

That night I prayed, "I am the clay, Lord, and you are the potter." I repeatedly turned to God during this trial. I desired to do His will.

April 18, 2011

Tim and Jane recruited a family friend to drive them to the Rochester airport for their departure today. The meteorologists forecasted a winter storm, and I wanted everyone to be safe in their own home. Ah, spring in Minnesota! Kathleen stayed home for a few more days, fearful that I might experience another seizure.

An orderly moved me to the ninth floor of the Sister Mary Brigh Building at Saint Marys Hospital on Monday of Holy Week. A nurse offered to give me a shower and shampoo. This simple gesture elated me. The water refreshed my spirit and body, but I hadn't realized how much these activities would wear me out. My lack of independence and privacy irritated me. I don't like it when people make a fuss over me. I prefer anonymity over the spotlight. At least I applied my own lipstick, L'Oreal's "Sea Fleur," without resembling a circus clown. Then I was ready for a nap.

Kathleen helped me eat lunch – a hamburger patty and carrots. I used a fork with my right hand. When you consider that I could barely move my right arm and hand twenty-four hours earlier, this was an accomplishment.

Brain cancer patients can't always tell when they need to go to the bathroom. I had a catheter inserted while in the ICU, but not when they moved me to the bed on to the medical ward. Using a bedpan intimidated me. Doctors wanted an accurate measure of my urine. The nurse called a member of the catheter team to my room. A technician operated a portable ultrasound device to scan my abdomen. I seldom emptied my bladder, so they inserted a catheter and drained my bladder. It was another indignity I had to endure. It mortified me when a nurse brought an institutional package of adult diapers to my room.

When I could get out of bed, the nurses helped me shuffle to the bathroom, a marathon of twelve feet. It took time to move the right foot in the correct direction. I made it to the bathroom and back. A nurse, Rachel, placed a luggage-style belt around my waist and assisted me in navigating a walker out into the hall. I felt like a dog being walked on a leash. Again, I experienced exhaustion by these tasks.

I measured my fatigue with a "carrot cake barometer." Any activity exhausted me and blunted my carrot cake intake to a bit of frosting. When I felt rested, I devoured a corner piece with the extra icing.

I learned to focus on my progress in small steps. I couldn't believe that I had been burning up the treadmill at the Dan Abraham Healthy Living Center (DAHLC) two weeks ago, and I missed my normal exercise routine.

Our friend, André, took Jim out to dinner, while his wife, Ann, stayed to visit with me. Jim might have lost more weight during the ordeal than I had.

After the visitors left, I needed my rest. The next day promised to be a big day for me. I would learn the final results of my brain biopsy. A physical therapist and an occupational therapist would plot my return to an active life. Overall, I continued to gain ground slowly. Things had slid downhill fast, but the recovery stuff was hard work.

I counted on the Lord, along with the prayers of family and friends, to help me recover and beat this illness.

April 19, 2011

Dr. Parney delivered the final pathology report on my brain tumor, "Mary, you have an Oligoastrocytoma, Grade III." Try saying that fast three times. Now I had a name for my nemesis.

"What does Grade III mean?"

"A pathologist looks at cells under the microscope to check for abnormal cells. They can range from a low Grade (I) to high Grade (IV). The Grade III tumors are actively reproducing abnormal cells. It is inoperable due to its location near the speech center and the part of the brain controlling your right arm and leg."

"Inoperable?" I murmured. His words shattered my world. I had trouble facing such uncertainty.

The unfamiliar terminologies overwhelmed me. Jim's medical training made communication easier between the doctors. I relied on him to make sure I received first class health care.

How could such an ominous enemy exist in me without producing symptoms? I struggled to think back and look for clues that might have showed something was wrong and came up empty on every attempt to recall any signs.

The Good: Dr. Parney continued, "The good news is that this type of tumor responds to radiation and chemotherapy. We are checking your tumor for a specific chromosomal abnormality called 1p 19q."

I wondered why an abnormality might be good.

Dr. Parney stated, "Some studies show better outcomes when a patient has this chromosomal abnormality. I am confident we can shrink this tumor. We will prescribe steroids to reduce the swelling in the brain. I think the weakness and seizures you are experiencing are related to the irritation in the brain from the biopsy."

His positive outlook appeased me. "When can I expect to start treatment?"

"The biopsy site needs to heal for about two weeks, so we will set up appointments for you to consult brain cancer specialists at Mayo over the next week."

Dr. Julie Hammack, a neuro-oncologist, made a special trip to Saint Marys to meet me. "There are some clinical trials available to you, but I suggest we follow the standard treatment. We don't want to delay therapy. The protocol calls for thirty-three rounds of radiation and six months of chemotherapy," she said.

"Why do you suggest I do not do a clinical trial?"

"Because we think we can shrink your tumor with the latest therapies. In a clinical trial, no one would know if you are getting the actual drug, Temodar, or a placebo."

"Is the chemotherapy a pill or intravenous?" I inquired. I have read of many nightmare stories about chemotherapy and its side effects.

"It's a pill. We will give you medication to ease the side effects of the chemotherapy pill. Prescriptions can be filled before you leave the hospital for the anti-nausea drug, Zofran, and your chemotherapy pill, Temodar. The prescription for Keppra should control your seizures. State law requires people to stop driving for six months following a seizure."

Ouch. There went my independence.

She caught my husband's attention when she said, "There will always be a treatment available for you."

That statement filled us with hope. It became clear Dr. Hammack was a strong advocate for my care and devoted to her patients. At this point, my prognosis was uncertain.

She told me, frankly, "You will never be cured." I exhaled like a deflated balloon given the severity of the diagnosis. My mind raced ahead to the question, "How much time did I have," but I was too nervous to ask. I prayed to do the will of God, no matter what He had planned for me.

The Bad: This was still cancer.

The Ugly: My silver hair would fall out, but living without hair didn't bother me.

Throughout the busy day, I had several visits from occupational and physical therapy. I relearned how to stand up from a chair and how to use a walker. Abby, my physical therapist, and I took two long walks. After exhaustive assessments, the entire health care team thought I would benefit from a five-day stay in the Mary Brigh Rehabilitation Unit at Saint Marys. I would be transferred there the following day. My family focused on the positive and encouraged me to do the rehab program.

I understood I would be busy there. I had to relearn how to dress, brush my teeth, use utensils, write legibly, navigate stairs, and develop the strength and skills I used to take for granted. The focus would be on safety, strength, and improving my health so I could go home. The rehab team warned me I would be tired, and I would not be up for visitors, as I concentrated my energy on recovery. The therapists suggested that Jim should bring me comfortable clothes. I gleefully accepted ditching the hospital gown but I wondered what outfit Jim might bring.

Receiving Holy Communion in the hospital gave me spiritual strength. I know with this great team of the Heavenly Father, doctors and the staff, family, friends and prayer warriors, I would conquer this enemy called Oligoastrocytoma.

CHAPTER 5

Hospitalization Rehab
April 20-25, 2011

April 20, 2011

The third floor staff on Mary Brigh oriented me to the routines of the Rehabilitation Unit at Saint Marys Hospital. I had a full day planned with the integrated therapies: occupational therapy (OT), physical therapy (PT), speech therapy (ST), and recreational therapy (RT). In addition, I had a consult with a social worker and a staff physician, Dr. Kenley Schmidt, in Physical Medicine and Rehabilitation (PM&R). I needed evaluations from each specialty to identify the goals I had to accomplish during my stay in rehab.

Each therapist went over the initial list of objectives to be achieved before discharge. The OT objectives resembled a kindergarten chart: be able to dress myself, tie my shoes, and feed myself; eventually folding the laundry and baking cookies would be added to that list. Mastering a daily journal was part of the ST duties. Walking without support was the goal of PT. With the help of this team I could re-learn each of those skills and move home, an achievement known in the rehab unit as "Independence Day."

Jim didn't want to miss out on the therapies, so he arrived early in the morning with clothing I needed for rehab – jeans, t-shirt, a fleece top, and tennis shoes. He brought the fleece top because he knew I didn't like being cold. He wanted to know what each therapist was covering so if I ran into trouble at home, he would know how to respond. If I suggested he leave, he assured me his place was with me. I didn't like being in the hospital with a controlled schedule. I resolved to be an excellent student in each therapy for an on-time dismissal. Jim brought me my iPhone therapist (IT) so I read the guest book entries on my CaringBridge site between therapies. This site offered an incredible gold mine of hope.

My first test was with ST and I wasn't worried. The task was to decipher a mixed-up calendar. Little did the therapist know she was dealing with the master of calendar organization! She handed me a journal to keep track of appointments, forcing me to make lists and practice handwriting. I shudder to think of my penmanship grade when I was in the hospital.

The ST would also say a series of words, and I had to repeat them. It required several tries for accuracy, but I eventually aced the quiz. There was no time to study for these exams, so this made me believe I was a pretty good student.

When my friend, Ann, came to visit, she brought an article, "True Confessions of a Recovering List-Maker." She knew my nature. The first sentences read, "Not long ago, I was reading an account about the sinking of the *Titanic*. A young crewmember rushed to the bridge of the ship and reported to the Captain, 'I'm afraid she is listing pretty badly.' The bad thing is I thought it was talking about me." This article forced me to laugh considering all the lists I wrote down: chores to be done, errands to run, groceries to buy, places to go, and books to read.

The RT needed to get an idea of hobbies I liked, so she requested that I compose an inventory of my favorite things. Roll the score from "My Favorite Things" from *The Sound of Music*. I liked traveling the globe with Jim, studying my faith, entertaining at home, exercising, sailing, snorkeling, and visiting with friends and family. The RT made notes that I liked to be active, creative and being with other people. Sitting still didn't appeal to me. I prayed I could return to an energetic life.

The social worker discussed the sudden changes to our lives and recommended support with names and agencies to help manage finances, health insurance claims, and resources related to psychological events. The American Brain Tumor Association (www.ABTA.org) was a good resource of information. We added appointments with our attorney and financial planner to our to-do list when I returned home. Change trickled down to Jim in the day-to-day aspects of life, such as bill paying. Since I had always washed and ironed Jim's white shirts, we sent his shirts to the dry cleaners. I let go of my control to clean the house when Jim hired Molly Maids. The Division of Nephrology and Hypertension and others gifted us a lawn service for the summer months, so it freed Jim from mowing on the weekends. We counted on dinners being delivered twice a week. We felt blessed by the kindness of others, and we didn't know everyone's names. Jim reduced his schedule at work to increase time with me. We told the social worker we were emphasizing the positive and adjusting to a "new normal."

April 21, 2011

I lost a sense of privacy in the hospital. While working together with patients and freely moving in and out of their rooms may be routine to the staff, it was an adjustment for me. The lack of privacy reminded me of when I helped to potty train Reagan while I was a Granny Nanny. She fully intended to do it herself, and yelled, "Privacy please!" Reagan and I had more than just our DNA in common.

The OT supervised me in the shower. I complied because I didn't want to have issues when I got home. The hospital bathroom was accessorized with grab bars near the toilet and in the shower. I brushed my teeth and applied my Sea Fleur lipstick. I dressed in the clothes that Jim had brought. When I dressed in street clothes, it gave me a feeling of normality. The OT suggested I sit on the bed to pull on my jeans instead of standing, in case I had any balance issues. She then noted that I could dress myself.

A new therapist named "Dr. Jack" arrived – canine therapy, K-9T. Dr. Jack worked as a Miniature Pinscher therapy dog that visited patients in the hospital. His friendly personality and prize-winning mug brought a smile to my face. I was on my way to OT in a wheelchair, but he scampered onto my lap. He posed for a picture as if he was a model for a magazine cover. Due to my busy itinerary, I couldn't visit Dr. Jack for long.

I had to re-learn how to use silverware during OT. My mind told me I was an adult, but I was learning juvenile tasks. With right-sided weakness, it was difficult to use a fork and knife to cut my food. This frustrated me to the point where I lost interest in eating. Just when I needed proper nutrition the most, my taste buds were worthless due to the medications I had to take. Using a spoon was the biggest challenge. My hands weren't steady. I trembled with each spoonful of soup so as not to spill as I ate. I wore food on my clothes, just like a toddler. Practice and patience became my mantra.

The RT took me to a room full of toys. We worked on coordination by testing my skills at shuffling blocks around. Who knew the hours I spent playing blocks with my grandchildren would assist me in rehab? I think I did pretty well in this skill test.

I was excited to get to the gym for PT because walking on my own was paramount for recovering and going on the pilgrimage to the Holy Land. The staff designed a program for me to walk again. Paul, my therapist, asked me to balance on a "wobble board," similar to balancing on a teeter-totter. We used a "BOSU˙ ball," like half an oversized beach ball, to regain my balance. These exercises were difficult with the loss of strength and stability on my right side. He encouraged me as he guided me through the paces of re-training the brain to use these muscles necessary to walk. I focused on stamina and endurance to finish the routines. We played catch with a balloon. My Granny Therapy (GT) of playing toss with a balloon came in handy. I learned to handle a walker at fifty-eight years old.

By midafternoon, my internal bell rang for nap therapy (NT). My psyche struggled to accept these new physical limitations. Jim seldom left me as he delegated his administrative duties from his laptop across the room. I drifted off knowing Jim's attentive nature would watch over me.

In the evenings, as the therapists went home, friends came to visit. They brought treats ranging from Carrot Cake Therapy (CCT), to Chocolate Therapy (CT) and Ice Cream Therapy (ICT). I had an over-sized sweet tooth. The nurses called my room "dangerous" because of the sugary indulgences. I must have mentioned I loved carrot cake on my CaringBridge site because carrot cake cookies and muffins arrived. Perhaps my carrot cake consumption led to a spike in carrot futures. I wasn't eating a normal hospital diet. My mother had been a dietician, so I had learned about healthy fare, but few foods, other than sweets, held my interest. Because of the drugs, my stomach refused most of the nutritious hospital cuisine.

Our pastor from the Church of the Resurrection, Fr. Kevin, arrived for a visit, and offered a blessing. Fr. Kevin informed me the congregation was praying for me. It comforted me to learn so many people were keeping me in their prayers. I don't seek the limelight, but hearing about the prayers on my behalf helped me transcend the adversity of a devastating diagnosis.

Nights in the hospital were lonely. I fell asleep easily around 10 p.m., but nurses paraded in and out of the room checking vital signs throughout the evening shift. Machines set off alarms when I rolled over on a tube. I prayed during these wakeful periods to further my relationship with God. He was my hope and salvation, and I yearned to do His will.

April 22, 2011

When I woke up, I remembered the day was Good Friday. I dedicated my rehab exercises to the Lord. He had died on the cross to redeem me; I prayerfully wished to align my sufferings to His.

Life in the rehab unit became routine within twenty-four hours. The OT arrived at 7 a.m. I showed her how I had mastered daily hygiene in the shower, getting dressed, and feeding myself.

I used the walker to go to ST. My pronunciation and word recognition had improved and I graduated from ST. It brought back memories of second grade and wanting to be number one in my class at recognizing consonants and vowels. I was on the fast track for dismissal.

The location of my hospital room made it convenient to the occupational laundry room and the occupational kitchen. The laundry room had a washer and dryer, along with detergent. They had piles of clean towels for patients to practice doing laundry. I didn't need instructions for doing laundry, drying, or folding. This was a chore I kept caught-up at home.

The occupational kitchen contained a refrigerator, stove and oven, and a sink. It took me back to a TV set sitcom. I made chocolate chip cookies following the directions on a package of cookie mix. I enjoyed baking because I ate the cookies fresh from the oven in my hospital room. The ability to do these tasks would be useful when I went home. Why hadn't I discovered this career of OT years ago? It hit my on buttons: baking and doing laundry.

In PT, Paul encouraged me to give up the walker and use a cane. As much as I aspired to re-learn to walk, I was unsure of myself. My strength and balance improved, but the cloud of doubt still hovered over me. Paul stood beside me with words of support. He taught me leg crossovers and a series of floor and standing exercises. We practiced going up and down steps. Sometimes, Jim persuaded me to walk with him around the unit for extra credit. I arrived in the rehab unit in a wheelchair, moved to a walker and graduated to the cane in two days. I credited my rapid improvement in PT to the years of exercising in the gym. My brain responded to the old brain waves I had used in exercise classes.

Late in the day, the team of the rehab unit did another assessment and determined I had earned two four-hour passes to go home on the weekend. I had to show Jim how I could maneuver around our house and use the skills I had acquired in the hospital. This excited me. I couldn't wait to be home even if for a short time.

Kathleen delivered a Good Friday meal of salmon, homemade mashed potatoes, and a spring fruit salad she had prepared. It was a delicious alternative to hospital food.

After dinner, I thought about Christ's death for my salvation. He used suffering and transformed the meaning of it when He died on the cross. I pondered on this ultimate sacrifice and sought strength from prayer.

I read Romans 5:1-5. *Therefore, since we are justified by faith, we have peace with God through our Lord Jesus Christ, through whom we have obtained access to this grace in which we stand; and we boast in our hope of sharing the glory of God. And not only that, but we also boast in our sufferings, knowing that suffering produces endurance, and endurance produces character, and character produces hope, and hope does not disappoint us, because God's love has been poured into our hearts through the Holy Spirit that has been given to us.*

April 23, 2011

I had to finish two therapies before I received my four-hour pass to go home today. When the OT came to my room, I had already showered and dressed, not waiting for supervision. I ate the hospital breakfast with utensils. My assignment for the morning was to do a load of laundry. I took the pile of clean towels, put them in the washer, added the detergent, pushed in the dial, and waited for the machine to finish its cycle. I transferred the wet towels to the dryer and set the control knob. Not complicated.

For PT, I walked with and without a cane. I did downward dogs from yoga. The rehab unit had a mock-up of a car door and seat, and I practiced getting into and out of the car. I had instructions to back up to the open car door, sit down, swing my legs around, and buckle up.

After the therapies, Jim took me home to assess what modifications would be necessary to prepare the house for my permanent homecoming. Some would be surprised to learn that Jim possessed the knack for home improvements.

Jim borrowed the luggage-style belt to put around my waist to help me get out of the car. He had the walker ready if needed. I could go up and down the stairs once a day while holding on to the handrail.

John, Lindsay, Reagan and Dylan returned to Rochester to celebrate Easter with us the following day. I don't think my grandchildren noticed a change in my physical characteristics, which differed from a healthy grandma. I was overly sensitive to how my body looked after the unending needle pricks for blood tests and IVs. Limits on my activities meant I couldn't lift the children or play on the floor. They accepted me as I was and were happy to see me. We spent the afternoon watching *Despicable Me* on a DVD. It kept my fretting attitude occupied and off my health issues. I had to go back to the hospital after dinner.

April 24, 2011

On Easter morning, I pulled on my pink bunny slippers and applied my L'Oreal Sea Fleur lipstick. Jim escorted me in a wheelchair to go to Mass at Saint Marys Hospital Chapel. It is no ordinary chapel: it looks more like a basilica, with marble floors and columns, stained glass windows, a white high altar with beautiful statues, and Latin inscriptions around the vaulted ceiling. John, Lindsay, Reagan, Dylan and Kathleen came to the hospital for Mass on this joyous day when we celebrated the Risen Lord who died for our salvation. Let Us Rejoice and Be Glad!

After Mass, we feasted on a delectable brunch that Kathleen had prepared at home. She produced a large white basket brimming with quiche, fresh fruit and homemade cranberry muffins. I spent time in Granny Therapy (GT) after the feast. My wheelchair became a playground on wheels and a source of entertainment to the grandchildren. They climbed on my lap, shared Easter treasures with me, and played with the drinking fountain in the lounge. They burned more energy than I did with PT. John and his family drove home after brunch at the hospital.

I returned to PT and OT before I could go home Easter afternoon. I planned to graduate on time.

My physical therapist noticed that I walked better without a cane: my strength was returning. I had to watch my balance. When I dragged my right foot, it showed I was getting tired.

On Easter afternoon, I earned another four-hour pass. Jim took measurements to install handicapped bathtub bars. While he worked in the bathroom upstairs, Kathleen and I watched one of our favorite movies, *The Sound of Music*. Afterward, she drove back to Madison, Wisconsin, and I went back to the hospital.

Between therapies in the rehab unit, I developed a closer relationship with God through prayer and meditation. I wanted to continue deepening that bond. I knew He was drawing me closer.

April 25, 2011

In less than a week, I passed my final exams in the rehab unit. I showed I had mastered each activity under every therapist's observation. It was commencement day, a.k.a., Independence Day. We learned good news about my biopsy. It revealed the tumor had a marker on chromosome 1p and 19q, which showed a greater chance of success in shrinking the tumor with radiation and chemotherapy. The information filled me with renewed determination to conquer this cancer. God had been good. To celebrate, we stopped for a milkshake on the way home.

I found out other things about myself while in the hospital. Being independent, to come and go on my own, was important. I needed that self-reliance back. I sought to be in control again.

As I reflected on my stint in the rehab unit, I realized there are no guarantees in life. I relied on my enduring faith to assist me to climb this cancer mountain. A pattern emerged as Christ walked beside me. Have trust in Him and give thanks for His blessings. God is the Great Physician.

CHAPTER 6

Out and In Again
Radiation and Hospitalization
April 26 – May 19

April 26, 2011

After my discharge from the hospital rehab unit, I continued outpatient appointments at Mayo Clinic. The next steps were: biopsy staples removed from my skull; meeting with my radiation oncologist, Dr. Stafford; and another Magnetic Resonance Imaging (MRI). This scan was necessary for making the radiation mask.

My sister-in-law, Ellen, recognized that Jim lacked fashion sense, and she sent me two comfortable fashionable outfits. I selected the teal and gray, layering a shirt, fleece and light spring jacket. The weather refused to recognize the calendar, remaining cloudy, rainy, and snowy.

Jim's parents, Joan and Mac, sent me new, trendy shoes to complete the outfit. The shoes looked good with jeans or workout attire. I was doing PT every day, so these would be useful.

Jim dropped me off at the Gonda Building in the Mayo Clinic complex where I received the red carpet treatment. Multiple polite, uniformed door attendants greeted me at the curb, assisted me into a wheelchair, and escorted me to the lobby while Jim parked the car.

I had never had a health emergency quite like this, so I entered the two-story foyer as a stranger. Despite my years darting in and out of Mayo buildings for one reason or another, I marveled with fresh eyes at the vastness of the marbled reception area. Patients of all ages and physical ailments sought the wisdom of those who helped others in a health crisis. We who live in Rochester are blessed to have the Mayo institution as a pillar in our community.

My first appointment was with Dr. Parney's nurse, Lucinda. She removed the staples from my biopsy incision. I squeezed Jim's hand, and Lucinda reminded me to breathe. I don't even like having a Band-Aid removed. The staples came out easily, not akin to wrestling staples out of paper. My skull was still tender from the biopsy. Lucinda wished me well for my next phase of treatment.

I met with my radiation oncologist, Dr. Stafford, and his nurse, Kristi. They discussed what to expect later that day when the MRI techs would create a custom mask for me. They needed exact measurements of where the radiation should be delivered. I would wear this mask during radiation. This didn't sound fun. Processing the medical jargon defied me. New emotions such as denial and fear surfaced as enemies because I was not familiar with the medical verbiage or what to expect. Words that were a foreign language a few weeks ago became the new norm.

Technicians crafted a thermal mold of my face and head. This flexible plastic mesh mask would become rigid when it dried. I imagine it would protect me if I ever played goalie in hockey.

MRI scans are not a pleasant experience, especially if you are claustrophobic. Thankfully, I am not. I was an expert in the machine due to prior back surgeries. I changed into a gown, and the technicians locked my clothes and jewelry in a locker. They asked a series of questions to make certain I had no metal on or in my body. An MRI machine uses magnetic fields of atoms to make images inside the body. Metal would be dangerous to me and the machine. I laid on a narrow padded table, they covered me with a warm sheet, resembling a pig-in-a-blanket. The technicians inserted earplugs to protect my hearing from the *chunk, chunk, chunk* of the machine. My head rested in a cradle on the MRI table while the techs covered my face with the newly made rigid mask. Even if I wanted to, I couldn't move. They gave me a bulb device to squeeze if I needed to come out of the contraption because some people react to the tight space and need a sedative. They talked and watched me from a window in the control room. A technician pressed the magic button, and I slid into the tunnel of the MRI. The ceiling of the machine was inches from my face, so I closed my eyes. I slowed my breathing and prayed as pinging noises bounced around my head. I kept searching for God's will to give me strength to beat this disease. So far, He had been directing my care.

Instead of forty-five minutes, the MRI scan took ninety minutes, challenging even a seasoned MRI veteran. These results would precisely localize the coordinates for the radiation to my tumor. I hoped I wouldn't get a bill for the extra time I spent in the machine. Luckily, I had great health insurance benefits. The Mayo bills came in the mail as fast as the greeting cards. Get well cards ran the gamut from humorous to religious. Comments written by the senders filled me with gratitude for the friendships I had.

At the end of the test, the MRI technicians came into the room and congratulated me on how well I did. They didn't tell me that my face resembled a miniature chessboard from wearing the mask for so long. If you go to Mapquest, I am sure you will find my brain coordinates there.

I made my way to the changing area, then out to the waiting room where Jim waited patiently. He smiled. "Do you need a wheelchair?"

I sighed and said, "Yes."

This must be how you feel after you have run a marathon.

Jim brought me home where I engaged in nap therapy (NT) at Command Central (CC), the family room sofa. Exhaustion set in from preparing for the radiation treatments.

Except for going up to bed at night or coming down in the morning, my restrictions were the main floor of the house. Jim insisted I call out for him when I wanted to use the bathroom in the middle of the night since I had fallen the first night home. It seemed impossible to rouse him, even though he slept next to me, just as it had when our children were infants. He asked me to walk hand-over-hand along the furniture for balance. He emphasized safety first.

April 27, 2011

Jim employed my friend, Allison, to babysit me when he went to the Dan Abraham Healthy Living Center (DAHLC) for a work out. Allison gave me a new name as I waged war with this tumor: Warrior Princess. Attacking the cancer empowered me. Allison and I logged on to our respective computers, and it was blazing keyboards. Jim asked me to stay quiet at CC. I used the time to compose my daily CaringBridge entry. Also, I found comfort reading devotional books.

Later in the day, I did OT, also known as the laundry. At this point, I embraced and savored mundane chores. My daily motto became, "Take nothing for granted." I assumed my pre-cancer lifestyle defined who I was. Now I didn't have the endurance to go for walks, to the gym, or to church.

Jim conducted my physical therapy with military precision. He demonstrated, and I followed the foot drills of crossovers and walking the line heel to toe, as well as bouncing a balloon in the air. I did "bird dogs" on my knees in the family room and had a balance routine of standing on one foot. We always ended with a waltz step. Jim and I had taken several dance classes over the years and we pretended we were Fred and Ginger. It felt right to be in Jim's arms.

April 28, 2011

Allison returned the next morning for the Royal Wedding of Kate and William. I set the table for breakfast using placemats and my everyday china. Allison brought fresh scones to feast on and a tiara for me to wear. We watched the television coverage of the regal event. I had toured Westminster Abbey, so I pictured the festivities in the church with its rich history.

May 1, 2011

I attended Sunday Mass at our parish, the Church of the Resurrection, for the first time since my April seizure. The second reading was from 1 Peter 1:3-9: *"Blessed be God and Father of our Lord Jesus Christ, who in His great mercy gave us new birth to a living hope through the resurrection of Jesus Christ from the dead, to an inheritance that is imperishable, undefiled, and unfading, kept in heaven for you who, by the power of God, are safeguarded through faith to a salvation that is ready to be revealed in the final time. In this, you rejoice, although now for a little while you may have to suffer through various trials, so that the genius of your faith, more precious than gold that is perishable even though tested by fire, may prove to be for praise, glory, and honor at the revelation of Jesus Christ. Although you may not have seen Him, you love him, even though you don't see Him now, but believe in Him, you rejoice with an indescribable and glorious joy as you attain the goal of your faith, the salvation of souls."*

This Bible passage had powerful significance for me. I read I might have to suffer through trials, but with the gift of faith, this illness would be for the glory of God. I honored God with my cancer. The message of salvation motivated me to get well.

May 2, 2011

Jim took me to my first radiation treatment. This was uncharted water. For radiation, I went into the vault, the name for the radiation room, not for the jewelry I wore. The thick walls prevented radiation from escaping. The masks lined up on the shelves reminded me of balls in a bowling alley. Were there that many people with brain cancer in Rochester?

Two technicians helped me onto the metal table for my treatment. For once, I didn't have to change into a hospital gown. I removed my glasses and earrings. They dimmed the lights and soft music played through speakers in the ceiling. It wasn't a spa, but it had a soothing environment. They fitted my custom mask over my face and head and locked it into place on the table. The table moved forward and backward to get the precise position. The radiation machine beamed a laser overhead and rotated around while the high dose rays targeted my malignant tumor. Technicians set the dials to the measurements taken at my last MRI. The machine used high-energy ionized radiation to damage the tumor so it would shrink. Healthy cells were resistant to radiation. This was a good time to pray, as my mantra was Phil 4:13, "*I can do all things in Him who strengthens me.*" I also prayed to Blessed John Paul II.

I left after a fifteen-minute treatment, the first of thirty-three sessions behind me. Jim indulged me with a frozen yogurt to celebrate my first radiation. I suffered no ill effects.

Jim drove to the pharmacy to pick up more Temodar, the chemo drug I would be taking while getting radiation. The cost of the drug overwhelmed me. I managed the monthly budget, and I noticed it looked like the Federal Budget, with many zeroes. Again, I felt blessed to have good drug insurance. I had no time or energy to itemize these new costs into our finances.

My friend and organizing angel, Lisa, arranged future rides to radiation with friends. It was a blessing to use the handicapped parking tag. Even with physical therapy, my strength and endurance had not come back to pre-cancer levels. My driver and I often went out for coffee (tea in my case) at a local coffee shop after my treatment. This allowed me to show my friends I appreciated their time with me. It distracted me from the cancer and opened my eyes that the rest of the world continued on with few concerns.

When my chauffer brought me home to Command Central, she prepared my noon meal and stayed until I went down for NT. My friend, Becky, drove me to a dozen of my thirty-three treatments. We had been good friends when our children were growing up. When

Becky learned I had brain cancer, she gifted me with a twenty-star quilt she made. The earth-toned colors matched my family room décor. Often Becky drove me home after the radiation treatment and brought me lunch of gourmet soup or salad she had prepared.

The clock regulated the schedule for the expensive medication. Jim designed a spreadsheet on the computer so I could make sure I was taking my drugs as prescribed. The highest number of pills was forty per day. I woke up at 5:45 to take my anti-nausea pill, followed by my chemo pill at 6:45. I usually had an early radiation appointment at 7:45. After radiation, I swallowed a dozen more pills. The time and spacing continued throughout the day and evening.

Jim bought one of those large, divided pill containers to help keep track of the medications. I think a fishing tackle box would have been more appropriate. Would he notice if I added an M&M or two?

I took an oral medication that was fluorescent yellow. Jim loaded a syringe for me every night just before dinner. The color made it hard to swallow. What else do we eat that is this color? Maybe a Peep at Easter? I was grateful to medical science that had formulated a successful drug therapy for cancer patients. The routine of taking the prescribed medication became habitual.

I met my medical oncologist, Dr. Buckner, who warned me I would be tired after radiation. Sleep would be essential; otherwise I would provoke more seizures and make the rebound difficult. I didn't want more seizures, so I devoted a couple hours in NT at CC every afternoon. Sleeping during the day was a luxury. My sister, Julie, told me fatigue was God's way of telling me to slow down. I accepted her wisdom.

I endured radiation Monday through Friday and didn't have therapy on the weekends. Staying home had its own rewards because I didn't have to be dressed for an early radiation appointment. I couldn't drive because of the seizures; I was on lock-down. However, the steroids made me want to dash out of bed like a racehorse at the gate.

In reality though, I had little interest in going any place. My days had changed drastically from the carefree come-and-go to the gym or errands. A new sense of duty to the treatments moved to the forefront if I intended to recover. Attacking the cancer empowered me.

In the mail, I received a card that read, "Jesus is a healer. His appointment calendar is never too full. His schedule is never too busy. His treatment is gentle, and His results are wonderful."

May 8-9, 2011

Kathleen surprised me by coming home for Mother's Day, despite being in the middle of final exams. Our Mother's Day tradition was to go out to Mayowood and walk the bluebell path. The periwinkle carpet was always a spectacular sight. Jim rented a wheelchair for this excursion so we could keep our ritual alive.

Before our outing, our neighbors, Carl and Teri, invited us over for a tea party on their porch. The normalcy of a social outing with friends on a spring-like day reinvigorated me.

When we came home, I lost my strength to stand, experiencing weakness in my right leg. The wheelchair stroll through the bluebells became instead an ambulance ride to the ER. I had a CT scan in the ER, but they couldn't find any changes.

The doctors guessed it was due to swelling of the tumor putting pressure on the brain, a reaction they expected from the tumor as it dies from radiation. Amazingly, this hospitalization didn't discourage me. They admitted me to Methodist Hospital, part of the Mayo Health Care System, where I continued radiation and chemotherapy. I had an important job to do: killing cancer cells. They added more steroids to my medications. After a two-day hospitalization, I went home, where I didn't stay long.

May 12-13, 2011

Jim rushed me back to the ER at Saint Marys Hospital three days later when I developed a fever of 104 and right-sided weakness. The doctor admitted me to the ICU for the night and treated me with antibiotics and more steroids. Jim slept on a cot in my room. The following morning, they transferred me to an oncology floor at Methodist Hospital.

Mayo Clinic is an integrated, outpatient clinic, where physicians see patients with rare diseases. It is known worldwide for its highly trained doctors. It is located in Rochester, Minnesota. Mayo employs more than 3800 physicians who provide the staff for the two Mayo-affiliated hospitals in town: Saint Marys and Methodist.

Mayo Clinic is a teaching institution, so when I was an inpatient at one of the hospitals, residents, interns, and staff physicians made rounds on me. Before daybreak, the most junior member of the health care team reviewed my hospital chart and then entered my hospital room. He appeared like a hologram at the foot of my bed and spoke in a low tone. "Good morning, Mrs. McCarthy. How are you doing today?"

I was never in a deep sleep, but I would startle and wonder where I was. Oh yes, the hospital. In a foggy state, I mumbled a reply until I assessed how I was doing.

My first thought was, "I am fine." Then the doctor asked me specific questions about the hospitalization. "Can you move your right arm?" I showed just how much or how little I could do.

"Can you move your right leg?" Again, I would show my ability to move my leg. Due to the location of my tumor, near the muscle center of the brain, the doctors needed to make sure the tumor wasn't growing and leaving me with any paralysis. The intern would make notes on my condition and return later with the staff physician.

On the heels of the early visit from the intern, our friend and neighbor, Tom, appeared with a large cup of steaming hot tea from Caribou. He is a transplant physician who came to the hospital early every morning. His quick wit brought me to life and forced me to laugh. He would retrieve my L'Oreal Sea Fleur lipstick so I would be presentable when the staff physician made rounds. Jim arrived around this time, and they exchanged opinions about the tests I needed or go over tests results.

The attending physician and his team of residents, students and nurses arrived before 8:00 in the morning. People paraded through my hospital room weighing in on my care. The doctors assessed my neurologic status using the techniques used in the Emergency Room. These included mental assessment like what day it was, could I follow their finger with my eyes as they moved it over their head, and how quickly I could tap my pointer finger to my thumb. The doctor reviewed my medications and outlined a strategy for dismissal. Just like that, they evaporated and moved on to the next patient.

Teams of doctors from Infectious Disease, Oncology, and Physical Medicine stopped by to consult on what caused the fevers. Jim made sure he was present when the staff made their rounds so he, too, could speculate the possible diagnosis. Jim was a nephrologist, the specialty known as "brainiacs." The nurses coined this word because of how this sub-specialty can see the whole picture in a medical crisis. I knew everyone had my best interest at heart.

I rode a gurney to multiple tests because I couldn't walk. To have no mobility of my own frustrated me. I had always been self-sufficient and now these frequent hospitalizations challenged me. I had no control over the situation that put me into the hospital. In fact, most of the time, I had no memory of the event that placed me there. When I woke up in the hospital, I had questions about my admission: Was it another seizure? Was my tumor swelling after the biopsy?

When I awoke in the ICU, it sent scary thoughts through my mind. Nurses checked my vital signs and followed the doctor's orders for medications and IVs. If my family was in the ICU room, their faces reflected grave concern, which fueled my panic. Luckily, I slipped back into a coma-like sleep while the nurses took care of me. I remembered the nurses in the ICU were fantastic. Doctors evaluated me before they moved me to a bed on the medical floor.

May 14-18, 2011

My brother, A.J., and my sister, Julie, drove up from Kansas City to bolster my disposition. We had expected I would be at home for their visit. They were good sports and came to the hospital every day with their laptops to stay busy while I disappeared for tests or radiation. They were a tonic to my shattered spirit. I showed my raw emotion with them, which was fear of, "what's next?"

What irritated me was that I could not count on what would happen in five minutes, five hours, or five days. I was willing to go through radiation and chemo, but the hospitalizations upset me. I was a planner and this out-of-control routine did not mesh with my personality.

My siblings advised me to "keep the faith," which had been one of my dad's mantras. My dad often quoted, "If you can't say anything nice about somebody, then don't say anything." Another insight into his spirituality was when he said, "Do unto others as you would have it done to you."

It comforted me to know both of my parents were in heaven interceding for me. My mom, who had had lung cancer, was my role model for my acceptance of cancer. I thought of her often. As the first of seven children to have a serious health issue, my siblings took responsibility for keeping my faith alive.

A.J. and Julie got me to laugh at old Cameron family jokes. The most memorable family joke was, "Why did the chicken cross the road?"

"Because he wanted to 'lay' it on the line." This referred to the widening of the state line near our house when we were growing up. We howled with laughter.

A.J., Julie, and I reflected on our mom's command of English and grammar. Mom had a talent for writing stories and poems. She shuddered when she heard any of us end a sentence with the word "at." I bought her the popular book, *Eats, Shoots & Leaves,* which covers proper punctuation. She enjoyed a chuckle or two from the book.

When my youngest sister, Julie, was born, my parents sent out family Christmas cards with the children depicting the Nativity scene. My older brother, A.J., was Joseph, and he wore a robe. I portrayed Mary, wearing a headscarf and Julie portrayed the Infant Jesus (in a cloth diaper). Angel wings adorned my sister, Ann. My three other brothers, Charles, John, and Joe, were shepherds. Costumes were simple with the shepherds wearing a towel draped over their shoulder and a broom handle for their staff. My parents' faith permeated our lives. I am not sure if a family picture in Christmas cards were the norm in 1961, but maybe our parents were trendsetters.

Jim and I knew many of the hospital staff as friends, so they told A.J. and Julie stories about Jim and me. The anecdotes always brought a robust laugh from everyone in the room. As the week went along and I felt better, my room had a party atmosphere from the hilarity of the tales exchanged.

My other siblings wanted to come to Rochester to visit me, but I held them at bay. As a control freak, I would think I should have to entertain and cook for their visit. A J. and Julie had to fend for themselves during their short visit to Rochester because I was in the hospital.

My friend, Kathy, a coordinator and supervisor in transplant, visited me in the hospital during the day. She had a heart of gold and wore a wide smile every day. I had to ask her one day, "Do I smell bad?" No one had offered me a shower, and I had not had the strength for it, but it bothered me. She replied, "No." When I reflect on the question, she kindly lied.

The pattern of each admission became familiar. I measured my progress by the method used to transport me to a test or appointment. First, there was the gurney. Since I could not use my right side, the medical staff transferred me to and from my bed with a silicone slider board. Several nurses on each side of the bed lifted me into the air for the transfer. Multiple monitor lines connected me to machines, so it became a bit of a tangled mess. Under other circumstances, it might have been fun to be thrown up in the air similar to a child's game of parachute.

When I was able to get in and out of my hospital bed on my own, escorts wheeled me to appointments, radiation, and physical therapy in the hospital. No one wanted me to fall, so they made sure PT covered each increment toward walking. As my strength returned, I used a walker, a cane, and eventually, a nurse held me with a luggage belt cinched around my waist. Over time, I walked by myself. What a real blessing to graduate a second time from PT.

The hospital stored heated blankets in a cabinet that looked like a bread warmer at a Subway sandwich shop. I requested them regularly as I was cold in the thin hospital gown. Each time I inhaled, I wondered if I would catch the wonderful scent of fresh baked bread.

My bruised arms looked like those of a drug addict. My veins collapsed after multiple needle sticks. The nurses tried half a dozen places on my arms and hands to extract blood or start an IV. They resorted to a pediatric size butterfly needle. My arms and hands resembled contemporary art with muted colors of purple, yellow, red, and blue.

Nurses dispensed medications around the clock per doctor's orders. They scanned my personalized jewelry, i.e., identification bracelet, for every little thing. Ka-ching!

The nurses always wore gloves when they came in the room to check my vital signs or dispense medication. However, my personal hygiene didn't seem to be top priority to the nurses during a health emergency. As I got stronger, I craved a shower. I remember one nurse named Grace. She was an angel. When I could tolerate a seated shower, she would gently caress my sick body and massage lotion over my weary bones.

Other shower experiences were not as pleasant. One nurse rubbed me down akin to a racehorse. When I felt healthier, I loved taking a shower by myself. I stood in the shower while the warm water soothed my mind and body. This was a step in the right direction for moving home. I couldn't wait to use the handicapped bars Jim had installed in our bathtub.

While I was in the hospital, Jim said his secretary, Sharon, had organized a group of friends that became known as "The Gardening Angels." They descending on our yard and went to work digging in our garden and in pots on our deck. The angels planted multi-colored annuals among my perennial flower garden. I couldn't get home soon enough to see the kaleidoscope of patterns and colors.

For Jim and me, this journey was like being seated in a rear-facing backseat of a station wagon. We didn't know the path or where the next bend would be on this voyage. We knew that when the ride stopped, we would be at our destination: the end of treatment.

I received a gift from Jim's secretary, Sharon, and her family, a Miraculous Medal on a chain. This medal had an image of the Blessed Mother on it with the inscription, "Mary, conceived without sin, pray for us who have recourse to thee." The medal signified Mary's promise of intercession at the hour of death. Our friend, Al, was going to Rome for a Papal audience, in the Clementine Hall of the Pope's apartment. He asked if I wanted him to take anything for Pope Benedict XVI to bless. I gave him my Miraculous Medal necklace, and the Pope blessed it.

I wear it as a testimony of my faith.

May 19, 2011

After a week in the hospital, the doctors decided my fever resulted from an allergy to a drug they had discontinued while I was in the hospital. They discharged me from what I hoped would be my final hospitalization. I had completed sixteen of the thirty-three radiation treatments during my time there.

A card arrived in the mail from a friend today. It read, "Happy the day the Lord has made. Let us rejoice and be glad!" I second that sentiment.

Jim remembered how much I liked to drive down Memorial Parkway in the spring when the lavender-colored crabapple trees bloom. He turned in that direction after picking me up at the hospital entrance. Who knows me better than Jim?

CHAPTER 7

The New Normal

Let's be honest. It's not every day you awaken and learn you have cancer. It is your reaction to the diagnosis that will guide you over the rocky road. Cancer is not something I chose to have, but I took ownership of how I would handle the disease. My new normal consisted of daily medications, radiation and physical therapy. There was no independence, no driving, and no going to Dan Abraham Healthy Living Center. Weekly blood draws caused my veins to collapse. The medication played havoc with my appetite and sleep. I was okay with losing my hair. I had to quit work, and my involvement in my parish plummeted. With all the negatives, I found myself being called closer to God.

I reflected back to 2006; my mother had lung cancer, and she accepted it with grace. She became my role model. She did not want chemotherapy, opting for quality of life over quantity. I became familiar with the seven-hour drive on I-35 between Rochester and Kansas City that year.

During my visits to her home, we always went out to dinner. Most of my siblings lived in the area, so they joined us. She called our outings, "*The Last Supper*." My mom had stopped her medications for arthritis, so we imbibed with her favorite cocktail, a martini with two olives. She recited familiar family history stories and kept a sense of humor. Her quick wit was evident when she mentioned one day about the long oxygen cord that allowed her to go any place in her apartment. She asked, "Do you suppose this (oxygen tube) is like the umbilical cord, only at the end of life?" Everyone had a good chuckle from the joke.

Now, I had this horrible diagnosis. My deeply rooted faith contributed to the strength I required as I developed a closer bond with God after the diagnosis. I grappled with fear and losing control, but they evolved into a catalyst for transformation. My mind ran wild with possible scenarios of what tragic events I could expect on this detour in my life. I didn't understand what was going on around me in the hospital. When I had a seizure, I blacked out and had no memory of what had taken place. Sometimes, I could not talk, and it frightened me. I felt like a bystander in a hospital scene.

When my speech returned, I was unsure of myself in my replies to the doctors. The doctors intimidated me by their education, and I didn't want the staff to think Jim had married a lunatic.

The thought of losing my balance kept me in bed. I cocooned myself in my own world, asking questions like, "What if I die?" Surely every cancer patient must have this question on their mind. It could happen. I had to wait and see what effects radiation and chemo would have on my brain tumor.

"What if I become paralyzed?" That idea terrified me. I enjoyed my freedom to come and go on my own. I wanted independence.

"When will I stop having seizures?" It frustrated me to wake up in the hospital after each seizure.

"What will Jim and our kids do without me?" I considered myself responsible for the home front, the day-to-day operations, and even long-term planning.

"Can I buy health insurance with a pre-existing condition?" I had good insurance, but insurance changes were on the horizon.

After personal pity parties, I pulled myself up by the bootstraps and learned to grow through this crisis. What might I learn from this experience? I would let God show me the way.

After nearly a month in the hospital, from the first trip to the ER and subsequent hospitalizations, I relished the freedom of being out of the hospital. Being home in familiar surroundings and not regulated by nurses and therapist duties liberated me.

I resumed outpatient radiation on weekdays. I could not drive because I didn't have a valid driver's license. My friend and neighbor, Lisa, organized all the chauffer services for the thirty-three rounds of radiation. Lisa color-coordinated a graph of names, phone numbers, and times of my drivers' help.

However, I had messed up Lisa's organization with the frequent hospitalizations. Now at home, I honored Lisa's efforts to offer me rides to radiation with friends. As I mentioned in the last chapter, my driver and I often went out for coffee or tea and a sweet treat before they brought me home to Command Central. Their positive energy gave me the strength I needed. These friends supported me when I desired it most. I cannot stress how much friends and family meant as they offered over one hundred percent of their time and energy.

Jim insisted I use a wheelchair when I went to radiation. I appreciated the wheelchair as my legs were still unsteady. My driver dropped me off at the west door of the Charlton Building, where a doorman helped me into a wheelchair. Then he called for an escort to take me to radiation, down one level, to Desk R.

Before one radiation appointment, I sat in the wheelchair in the lobby. My radiation oncologist, Dr. Stafford, rounded the corner. I recognized him by his large frame and commanding presence. A teddy bear personality encircled him. He grinned when he realized I was out of the hospital. "I am delighted to see you coming to radiation as an outpatient." We exchanged pleasantries and then he asked, "Is Jim parking the car?"

"No. I am waiting for an escort."

Dr. Stafford laughed and bellowed, "I can take you to radiation." He told the person sitting at the control desk, "Cancel the escort." He wheeled me to my appointment! All the eyes in the waiting room centered on us as we entered. Dr. Stafford surprised the radiation desk staff as they saw him steer me to radiation. My heart fluttered. I doubt if many patients find this level of personalized service at their hospital.

My cancer journey forced me to recognize another reality: the loss of my hair. I had heard about this side effect from radiation and chemo, but I could not imagine my response. Jim said he loved me with or without hair, and he took me to purchase new silk pillowcases because he had heard they would be nicer for my head.

I accepted my hair falling out, even though it made me look sickly. It was a strange sensation. As I fell asleep every night, I visualized an army of Pac-man figures marching through my scalp, nibbling at my roots.

When I woke up in the morning, there was hair on my pillow from the late nighttime battles. Many people have physical challenges, and this was just hair. I saw the public in a different light and had more empathy for those whose needs were larger than my own.

Six weeks after my diagnosis, I summoned the energy to apply blush and mascara along with my daily application of Sea Fleur lipstick. My companion, Imelda, drove me to an appointment with my hair stylist, Gayle. I hobbled into the home salon where everything looked familiar. Current magazines and new fashion hairstyle books adorned the tiny shop. It would be a long time before I could avail myself of those resources. Gayle had been my hairdresser for the past thirty years and she was giving me a buzz cut.

I reminisced on my friendship with Gayle. When Kathleen was pre-school age, she accompanied me to the salon. At home, Kathleen played "Gayle." I laid on the sofa and she combed and brushed my hair. It relaxed me. At her young age, she carried on a pretend, grown-up discussion, asking, "How is Kathleen doing?" I smiled, listening to her repeat the conversations between Gayle and myself. I thought about those happy memories as I sat in the swivel chair facing the mirror.

Gayle covered me with the purple plastic sheath and pulled it snug around my neck. She fired up the clippers and soon my gray hair fell to the floor. I was comfortable having Gayle do this. She shaved the obliterated Pac-man figures that had been crawling through my hair and in my dreams. The close-cropped style showed my still healing biopsy scar. Having my head shaved wasn't as traumatic as I thought.

Gayle, herself, was a cancer survivor. She ordered a pink turban for me. I brought several long neck scarves and bandanas to the appointment and she showed me how to wear them. Before my cancer, I seldom wore hats or visors because of how they matted my hair. Now I embraced them as both a fashion and cancer statement. Since it was summer, my head was not cold. Life was easier when I didn't have to factor in time for blowing my hair dry every day.

I put styling visits aside for now. I had to find a temporary solution. My friend, Becky, picked me up to go buy a wig. Kathleen met us at the wig store. The manager showed the proper way to wear a wig. We shared many laughs as the clerk tried wigs on me in an array of styles and colors. I had colored my hair for many years, so I handled a wide range of hues, but I never ventured as far as pink or blue. When the shop owner put on a brunette bob, we all knew it was a winner. It resembled the color of my natural hair when I was in my twenties.

With my hair ordeal settled, I realized I still cared about my appearance. Kathleen hosted a spa night for me when she came home from college. She filled my handicapped-accessible bathtub with warm water and a sachet with lavender and tea tree oil. The herb-infused tub felt delightful to soak in. The pincushion bruises on my arms after my hospital stays didn't bother me. The soothing music of Josh Groban played on her iPod, a thoughtful gesture. I had lamented to Kathleen earlier in the week that I couldn't risk an infection from a pedicure in a salon. She spent an hour giving me a French tip pedicure when I got out of the tub. I was ready to be seen in public again.

It was an opportune time to realize how blessed I was. Sure, I was reeling from the shock of having cancer, but the goodness of others shone through. I believed God wanted me to slow down and appreciate life. I began to re-order my priorities, and I focused on the growing relationship with God.

After a relaxing soak, I had no trouble falling asleep. Jim had started a nightly ritual when we went to bed where he placed his hand on my biopsy scar and said the Hail Mary. He was a man of faith and he asked God to deliver me from this cancer. I dozed in heavenly bliss.

Drifting to slumber was easy, but difficult to stay asleep all night. This wakefulness was a side effect of the high doses of steroids the doctors used to reduce the swelling of my brain. Mr. Sandman visited me around 10 p.m., but I wasn't able to stay in dreamland for over four hours. When I awoke, I tried not to disturb Jim. I reached for a pen and paper that I kept near the bed to make notations for the next day's CaringBridge entry. My attempts to be discreet were not always successful, because Jim often said, "Mary, put the pen down." I knew that he was serious, but what can you do when you are wide awake at 2 a.m.? The funny thing was, I was only scribbling gibberish in the middle of the night. Here I assumed I was being profound! After making notes, I attempted to get back to sleep, but instead I rolled and turned resembling a rotisserie chicken at Sam's Club. The doctors prescribed several sleeping pills to help me sleep through the night. Nothing bridged the four-hour cat nap between 10 p.m. and 2 a.m., and dawn.

As my strength returned, Jim allowed me to move to another bedroom when I woke up in the middle of the night. Much like Goldilocks, I searched for a bed that felt just right. I relaxed and turned on a light and read a devotion or two. Sometimes, I even ventured to the main floor and switched on the TV or a CD for quiet meditation. Usually, I drifted off as the sun came over the horizon, but that peaceful moment would always be interrupted by the first dose of medication for the day.

I discovered a finer appreciation for God's nature, and because I couldn't sleep, my senses were on alert. In the calm of the pre-dawn day, I heard the chatter of the birds. I imagined conversations in their lyrical tweets. Birds were sending out tweets long before they become popular through social media. After preening, they flew off to find worms for their babies. Human nature is not that different from other species, but we have the knowledge of who crafted us in His image.

I had always been too busy to stop and acclaim the gifts that God had given me. He was the Author of Nature. The early hours at Command Central allowed me to take in the glorious sunrises. The giant yellow orb in the sky rose on the eastern horizon and took my breath away. I absorbed the Technicolor of summer as the heavens went through their kaleidoscope of colors. The vibrant plantings by the Gardening Angels swayed in the breeze. Soft lilac fragrance from the bushes next to the house wafted in through the open windows. It was Mother Nature's air freshener.

Another side effect of radiation was a phenomenon known as "chemo brain." This term defines a cancer patient's difficulty with thinking and memory. Confusion and cognitive reasoning were symptoms of chemo brain. I became upset when I couldn't be understood. Most people realized that I wasn't at the top of my game and offered me a wide berth in my communication skills.

I had trouble concentrating, especially made clear when I attempted to balance the checkbook. I am a to-the-penny kind of girl. Another time, I failed to recall the location of the Mississippi River. I struggled to picture a map and the route to Chicago from Rochester. I realized we crossed the Mississippi River on our commutes to Chicago, but did we drive east or west? This inability to remember basic points of origin troubled me. Further incidents with chemo brain came when I addressed an envelope and questioned where the stamp went.

My family used to tease me when I made up words: Maryisms as they became known. I did this before I learned I had cancer. The family still won't let me forget the time I said, "The debris was *sprewn* around" instead of, "the debris was strewn around." It wasn't comical during a conversation with a professional, either a doctor or a nurse. I answered a question with what I regarded was the correct word, but it was not. That embarrassed me.

As I hunkered on the family room sofa, I saw chores I had always done, but were now off limits. The restrictions didn't mesh with my personality and discouraged me. The seasons had changed, and I hadn't moved my winter clothes out of the closet to allow room for my summer wardrobe. I intended to be independent and active again, so I had to learn to let go before I moved on.

I wrestled with the timing of this disease. The discovery of cancer canceled our trip to Vancouver. Now, I ruminated over the deposit we had made for a pilgrimage to the Holy Land in January 2012. Cancer knocked on my door at an inconvenient time. I needed to be well again, both physically and mentally.

In the radiation lobby, pamphlets hung on the racks describing various cancers. Most of the titles I looked through had to do with brain cancer: the variety and types of tumors, treatments, etc. The brochures that interested me were the ones that spoke to the spiritual well-being of people with cancer. I was aware from my private spiritual journey that my religious beliefs sustained me. I trusted in God. One of the booklets encouraged cancer patients to share personal writings. This was easy for me to do through my CaringBridge site as I maintained up-to-date entries on my physical and spiritual health. I sought to be a source of strength and hope to others.

A message in a get-well card I received read, "There is comfort in God's presence and healing in His light. God is like a candle aglow in the night, showing the way with His comforting light, urging us onward, whatever's before us – shining with promise to heal and restore us."

CHAPTER 8

A Reprieve

I completed the thirty-three rounds of radiation, along with the oral chemotherapy drug, Temodar, on June 14, 2011. Funny as it sounds, I would miss the routine of going to Desk R and seeing the dedicated technicians. They became my friends over the past six-and-a-half weeks. They educated me on the purpose of radiation; explained the odors and lights I experienced as normal; supported me by asking how I was doing; encouraged me to keep napping.

A radiation tradition had spread throughout the country. It began in 1996 at M.D. Anderson when a Navy Rear Admiral, who had head and neck cancer, installed a brass bell at the radiation center in Houston. He intended for patients to ring it when they completed their therapy.

I saw and clapped for patients when they had completed their radiation at Desk R. When I came back to the waiting room after my last treatment, I approached the bell that hung on the wall, and struck it three times. It symbolized the restoration of balance, harmony, and life-energy. I experienced a sense of accomplishment. The people there, waiting for radiation, or who were there as support to someone receiving radiation, applauded my success. To mark the end of radiation, I brought a cookie cake and balloons to recognize the staff.

I had a follow-up appointment with my oncologist a week later. Jim accompanied me to the doctor's office on the eighth floor of the Gonda Building. I was eager to find out what to expect next.

Dr. Buckner and Yvette, his nurse practitioner, entered the room. They greeted us with smiles. I loved hearing Dr. Buckner speak in his southern accent. He drew out each word. He possessed a gentlemanly and professional demeanor. "How are you doing today?"

"I am doing well. All the family will return to Rochester to celebrate the end of radiation. We will have no vacant rooms."

Dr. Buckner smiled. He made eye contact with me as he described the chemotherapy to treat my oligoastrocytoma brain tumor. I scribbled notes in an attempt to take ownership of my disease and understand the details.

"I have returned from the International Oncology meeting in Chicago. The treatments I recommend are the most current and up-to-date therapies being used for a patient with your type of cancer. We will prescribe Temodar, the same medication you were taking during radiation, but this dose will be two-and-one-half times stronger than the dose you've been taking," he explained.

"What's the timeline for chemo?" I asked while I pondered the much larger dose of chemo.

Dr. Buckner leaned back in his chair, "The standard protocol for Temodar is taken over six months. A cycle is five days 'on' and twenty-three days 'off.' If we start the drug in mid-July, you could complete the chemo by early in 2012."

I became alarmed. I'd come to the appointment with a calendar. Jim and I had a pilgrimage planned to the Holy Land in early January of 2012. I studied the calendar. "If chemo starts on July 12th," then I moved out and circled twenty-eight days later, "then the second of six rounds of chemo would start August 9th." I regarded the doctor's puzzled face.

Sitting at the desk with the computer in front of him, he spun around to discuss the chemo with me. "Chemotherapy is a blend of science and art. I can't tell you that you will start the next round of chemo every twenty-eight days. We have to check your platelets before every round. You might need to wait five weeks or more between treatments."

I wanted to cry, but I hid that emotion from Dr. Buckner. I must finish chemo before our pilgrimage, just over six months away. Here I was, wanting to be in control again.

"The platelet count is important," Dr. Buckner insisted. "Platelets are specific kinds of blood cells that prevent bleeding. The body's ability to produce platelets is diminished when a person is on chemotherapy. That puts a patient at risk for bleeding."

Platelets or not, I made up my mind to be finished with chemo by Christmas.

"You must listen to your body when you are on chemo. There will be periods when you are extremely tired. If you don't rest you will be at risk for seizures."

The thought of more seizures frightened me. I made a mental note to nap when needed. Dr. Buckner did a brief neurologic assessment: I followed his finger with my eyes, he tested my muscle strength, I walked the line for a balance check, and he hammered my reflexes.

I left the appointment with a month of freedom from structured schedules. My top priority: to regain my strength and stability over the summer. Kathleen would be home from college and act as my physical therapist to help reach my goal. We started daily one-mile walks in our subdivision. Kathleen became my motivator.

After our walks, we moved inside and did leg crossovers, walked the line (much like a sobriety test), and batted a balloon back and forth. In the family room, we did floor exercises of planks, downward dogs, and leg lifts. I missed my classes at Dan Abraham

Healthy Living Center that had included some of these strength and balance routines.

Celebration

After I finished radiation, our children, spouses, and grandchildren returned for a short holiday to celebrate the end of radiation. I felt better for this visit than I had during the biopsy visit in April. At a time like this, just being surrounded by family was tonic for my soul.

Kathleen prepared the house for visitors. She liked to leave vacuum marks on the carpet. John instructed his children, "Go into the living room, and lie down on the carpet. Raise your arms over your head and spread your legs like you were making snow angels." He said this just to irritate Kathleen. Reagan and Dylan loved the idea of carpet angels.

Reagan and Dylan moved to the family room and drew in Cousin Emma for a costume party with princess dresses that we had accumulated. Even Dylan joined in wearing a dress. That would serve as blackmail when he goes to high school.

Jim had climbed the stairs to the attic over the garage and retrieved the toys we saved. He washed the items on the deck and brought them inside. Jim stretched out and played with the grandchildren. The Fisher-Price dollhouse captivated Reagan and Emma's playtime, while Dylan preferred the Matchbox cars. I rested on the sofa and observed the growing relationship between grandfather and the three tots.

Soon the three grandbabies moved outside to frolic. They joined the neighborhood children on their swing sets. Meanwhile, their dads, Tim and John, drew chalk animals on the driveway, attracting a crowd.

Emma entertained us at mealtime as she did not like dirty hands, so she asked for a cloth to wipe them. Reagan and Dylan consumed their finger food freely. After lunch, they had energy for a stroller ride to a nearby park with their parents. The trio liked to swing and play on the slide. I snoozed while they were away.

Lindsay and Jane are great mothers, and they enjoyed each other's company. The 2,000-mile distance between Minnesota and New York made visits difficult for the young families. Dinner brought a self-service buffet, keeping food allergies in mind. Both Reagan and Dylan had peanut allergies. Our three-season porch off the kitchen worked well for *al fresco* dining. We managed adult conversation, although I can't recall what subjects were covered over the shrieks of the wee ones.

At the end of the day, it was bath time. There was no limit on bubbles at grandma's house so there were squeals of delight. Bath time resembled the rub-a-dub three-men-in-a-tub. The grandkids had fun putting on soapy mustaches and beards offering prime photo ops.

Before bed, the three cousins relaxed on the sofa in their jammies and watched a DVD. We had no issues getting them to bed. They had used up their energy. I wasn't far behind them. A sense of love and gratitude washed over me for the nucleus of family.

**

After the families departed, I had a series of dental appointments for a root canal. I had displaced my two front teeth during my first seizure in April. While I didn't look forward to the dental procedure, I looked forward to being able to bite food with my front teeth. No more thinking I was Dracula. My friends called to offer chauffeur service to the dentist, and I gladly accepted.

**

During the month between the end of radiation and the start of chemotherapy, the doctors weaned me off the high dose of steroids. I had had no seizures since May. I had been on doses as high as 40 mgs. of Dexamethasone – an industrial strength to those unfamiliar with steroids. The doctors prescribed the steroids to reduce the brain swelling from the biopsy and radiation. Steroids brought on unlimited energy, but also sleepless nights. Doctors eased me off the steroids gradually. I considered myself a deflating helium balloon. Drowsiness replaced the predawn energy surges. I changed from a Tasmanian devil with lots of energy, to Mrs. Rip Van Winkle at Command Central.

**

We took advantage of one of Jim's summer vacation days, and drove to Nelson, Wisconsin, about ninety minutes northeast of Rochester. Kathleen accompanied us. I took a nap while Jim navigated the winding country roads. Nelson is a scenic little town known for its dairy and cheese store. We purchased a picnic lunch in the deli and continued on for about an hour to Maiden Rock, near Stockholm, Wisconsin, and a site high above the Mississippi River. Fluffy white clouds floated across blue skies on a perfect summer day.

We enjoyed lunch on a blanket in the clearing. After the meal, we sprayed ourselves with bug spray and sun tan lotion, then hiked to the bluff. The trail started under a canopy of dense trees. We spotted plants of coral bells, daisies, black-eyed Susans, ferns, reed grass, and raspberries. Over the bluff, we saw peregrine falcons and turkey vultures soaring, while sailboats tacked and came-about in the Mississippi water below. We sipped long drinks from our water bottles as we admired the tranquility.

On our hike back to the car, we wished we had left a trail of breadcrumbs like Hansel and Gretel. The three-foot-tall grass made the outing quite an adventure. "Which way do we turn?" we asked each other.

We came back to our car laughing about hiking "off trail." A stop at the Dairy Queen in Wabasha completed our day. I drifted to sleep for an overdue nap as Jim chauffeured us home.

Ready for Chemo

Dr. Buckner scheduled another MRI, with a blood draw for a platelet count, on July 8, 2011. The staff needed to know if the radiation had any effect in shrinking the tumor. The Mayo Clinic was a great place to be as a cancer patient because you can have your MRI and blood drawn in the morning and get the results that afternoon. Dr. Buckner had previously warned me, "The MRI results might look worse than the original scan taken in April, due to the swelling of the brain from radiation."

Jim and I were learning the rhythm of my chemotherapy appointments. We made it a date day. It started with blood work and then the MRI in the morning. Then we ate lunch at one of the restaurants downtown. Jim seemed to know everyone, and they offered us greetings and family support.

In the afternoon, I had my appointment with Dr. Buckner. Jim and I sat on the familiar sofa in one of the exam rooms on the oncology floor. Yvette came into the exam room with a smile. Even though I was older than Yvette, she offered the motherly care I sought and I appreciated her concerns. "How are you feeling?" she asked.

"Fine." I wasn't feeling great, but I was okay. "I'm ready to start chemo."

She did a brief neurologic exam while discussing the weather and our day trips. It wasn't long before Dr. Buckner walked into the room and shook my hand. He took a seat at the desk and turned on the computer.

I held Jim's hand. I was nervous for the results from the MRI. "There has been a substantial reduction in the size of the brain tumor," Dr. Buckner exclaimed. Grinning, he turned the computer toward me so I could see the scans on the monitor. I don't know who had a bigger smile, me or Dr. Buckner.

"You see how the tumor has shrunk because of radiation? We hope to shrink it further with chemo," Dr. Buckner added.

There wasn't much need for further discussion. My tumor was shrinking! The radiation had proved worthwhile. I captured a picture on my phone of the MRI image of my shrinking brain tumor. I intended to remember the joy I felt that day. There were high-fives all around. Dr. Buckner performed a brief neurologic exam, and I passed all the tests. I was on cloud nine.

On our way out of the clinic, we filled the prescription at the subway pharmacy for more Temodar. Mayo Clinic became a beacon of hope for me. We said a short prayer of thanksgiving for the radiation.

We dashed home. Our friends, Nancy and Phil, had gifted us with four tickets to the Josh Groban concert in Minneapolis that night. Kathleen and her friend, Angela, joined us. I spent time on the drive to Minneapolis calling family and friends with the good news: the tumor showed signs of shrinking, and chemo would begin on July 12, our thirty-sixth wedding anniversary. What an ideal gift! We had time for a celebration at the Hard Rock Café across from the Target Center before Josh took the stage.

Our friends, Ann and André, had given us a gift certificate to the historic St. James Hotel in Red Wing, Minnesota as a Christmas gift. The city is one hour northeast of Rochester, on the Mississippi River. The hotel maintained the 1900's style with antique furniture, ornate lighting, period wallpaper, and old photographs, giving an impression of luxury from a bygone era. Months before, I'd made a reservation to celebrate on the weekend before our thirty-sixth wedding anniversary, so we headed up on July 9th.

Jim and I roamed the neat and tidy streets of the small town and ambled down to the levee. We could picture women and men in the fashion of that time boarding steamboats on the Mississippi.

We returned to the St. James for our dinner reservation in a dimly lit, lower level restaurant. The food tasted first class, but I was too tired to enjoy the feast. I was ready for bed shortly after dinner because I skipped my nap.

I started chemotherapy drugs on our anniversary, July 12, 2011. There were no ill effects the first few days of taking the drug. That changed on about day three. The nausea challenged me as it did when I was pregnant. I called Yvette, the nurse practitioner, and she gave me the green light to add another half tablet of an anti-nausea drug (Zofran) in both the morning and evening. The nausea ruined my appetite. I survived on saltine crackers, despite the wonderful meals that friends delivered to our home. I needed strength to fight the cancer cells battling in my body. After five days of the chemo drug, I had twenty-three days to recover.

The CaringBridge site offered a way for family, friends, acquaintances, and strangers to share their prayerful support and offer me encouragement. In turn, I used the site to thank the drivers who took me to and from daily treatments, waited with me during the day, and provided Jim and me with healthy and flavorful meals. As a list-maker, I couldn't keep up with the services and gifts that family and friends showered on me. I continued to pray to Blessed John Paul II and asked him to intercede on my behalf for a miracle cure to my brain cancer. I was full of faith, hope and love.

Two powerful words, with which I began my daily prayers, were "trust" and "thanksgiving." I prayed for trust to do His will throughout my day, and I was thankful for the blessings He had given me. It bummed me to have cancer, but I prayed God would have a positive outcome for me.

CHAPTER 9

Round 1

Chemoade

When life hands you lemons, make lemonade. I didn't get lemons. Instead, life handed me chemo, so I made chemoade, which is much more bitter.

The goal of the chemotherapy drugs was to stop the tumor growth by preventing cell division. Temodar was a systemic chemotherapy drug that traveled through the body via the blood. It crossed the brain barrier into the tumor cells and destroyed them.

Unfortunately, the effects of the drug the doctor prescribed left me nauseated and listless. I thought the powerful medications might destroy me.

An increase in Zofran addressed the nausea, but that led to constipation. I lived in agony. Adding fiber and drinking liquids did little to keep things moving. I required bigger artillery. I stirred Miralax into beverages so often that I considered investing in their stock. This concoction offered slight relief.

My energy level remained low compared to the days on steroids. Kathleen and I pushed through physical therapy walks at dawn, then came inside to do strength and balance exercises. One morning we walked too far and had to call a friend to come get us.

After completing a workout, I returned to Command Central. Eventually, I learned to listen to my body and understand the chemo cycle.

Chemo, like radiation, intensified the senses. Certain smells, such as cooking meat, were still troublesome. It added to the nausea. However, when my appetite returned, meat suited me. Angels delivered meals ready to pop into the oven. Birds woke me up with their chirping, and I drank in the beauty of nature in the vibrant flowers in our yard.

I used fewer drugs, so that reduced visits to our household medication vault. So far, weekly blood counts had remained in check – splendid news as I waged war with those nasty cancer cells. I wanted the platelet count to stay high so I could finish chemo before Christmas and travel to the Holy Land in January, 2012.

I survived in a state of confusion, never sure of what would happen next. Friends supported me and struggled alongside me. They attended to my need of reassurance I could expect a good outcome. Networks of people helped me address my emotions and uncertainty through talk-therapy. This turmoil did not mesh with my personality. It was essential I made the most of every day.

I longed to do mundane chores such as the laundry and dishes. I had passed the occupational therapy exam when I had been in the hospital, so I considered myself capable of doing these things. Kathleen did these chores when she was home for the summer. Jim took his shirts to the dry cleaners. I had always preferred to do the ironing myself because I didn't like the starch the commercial dry cleaners used.

Kathleen excelled in housework, which meant she knew how I liked things cleaned. I wished I had the energy to dust and vacuum. One day, my friend Ann, came and cleaned the house for me while Kathleen had another obligation. Ann does not enjoy cleaning, yet she willingly offered to come over and dust and vacuum. If I graded her efforts, they would be A+.

The summer warmth bathed me in its sunshine when I sat on our three-season porch. The porch suited visitors as well. I had lived in Minnesota for thirty-four years, but I could not get the cold out of my body.

Seven faith-filled families lived on our cul-de-sac. We often hosted a summer picnic on our driveway, and Lisa and Scott hosted an annual Christmas dinner with a gourmet meal. Another Scott popped delicious popcorn and brought it over frequently. Angie and Tom lived next door with their four children. I got to know Angie's parents who often came to visit. One day when I was outside, Angie's dad, John, came over to inquire how I was doing. He wove his faith into our conversation. As he was about to leave, he asked me if he could bless me. I readily accepted his blessing with tears streaming down my face.

Practicing my Catholic faith became paramount during this cancer journey as I relied on God. I attended Sunday Mass at our parish, Church of the Resurrection, and parishioners offered welcome smiles. Jim guided me by my elbow to our pew. It provided an opportunity to rest in God's arms. I listened intently to the gospel reading and did not fall asleep during the sermon. I wasn't keen on the focus on me due to physical changes of the wig, weight loss and unsteadiness in my gait. Some of the worshippers did not know what to say to me, and I found it to be an awkward situation.

I formulated a slate of questions to ask my oncologist at the August appointment. These included concerns with insomnia, fatigue, constipation, mild right-handed weakness, and dragging my right foot. I looked for assurance that the side effects were normal. I needed to erase the fears and doubts that lurked in my mind. The image of the shrinking tumor on the last MRI fueled my determination to get well during round one of chemotherapy.

Summer

Garrison Keillor, author and humorist of *The Prairie Home Companion,* had a radio show on Minnesota Public Radio set in mythical Lake Wobegon, Minnesota. He often started his broadcast with an update on the weather. I will follow his lead. It was July now, so you could count on days and nights to be hot and humid. The 10,000 lakes drew natives and visitors to Minnesota. Although we don't own a cabin up north, friends invited us to their place for our summer fix at the lake, but we declined. Every age found enjoyment in the cool and refreshing waters. Summer transformed the playground of activities to revolve around powerboats, pontoons, and jet skis.

We relished the longer days with sunshine after dinner. Other options to stay comfortable in the hot weather included going to the movies, retail therapy, or eating out. To escape the heat, we saw the latest Harry Potter movie, *Deathly Hallows*. Even if you have not followed the lightning-bolt-scarred wizard over the past ten years, I recommend the movie for the special effects and action.

Day of Beauty

I belonged to a girls club in Rochester whose name comes from the TV show, *The View*. Marianne, Katie, Kathy S., Kathy E., Ann and I were the charter members. We gathered at Panera for our bimonthly meetings. It was a chance to bolster each other and offer a social outing. These women acted as second mothers to Kathleen during her childhood and now into her college life. A week after my initial round of chemo, Kathleen held a "Day of Beauty" for the five "View" girlfriends at our home. She included Becky, who had been my chauffer to most of my radiation treatments. Kathleen sent out an email invitation to this support team with a basic 12-Step Guide for makeup application.

Kathleen brought her beauty supplies to the kitchen table. She showed and narrated each step in a two-hour demonstration. She knew how to apply cosmetics in up-to-date colors. This "how to" presentation took us back to the '60s and '70s.

"Remember when we wore blue eye shadow from the eyelashes to the eyebrow?" A chorus of "Yes," rose up.

"When I was in high school, I plastered liner and thick mascara on my eyes," Kathy exclaimed. It jolted everyone into reflecting on our sisterhood. The hippie era focused on dramatic cosmetics.

"Remember the hair styles like Farrah Fawcett?" She starred on the TV show *Charlie's Angels.* Girls transitioned to a natural look with less eyeliner and eye shadow, and neutral lip gloss by the mid '70s.

Kathleen had prepared a delicious luncheon of chicken salad and croissants, served in the dining room after her tutorial. Ice tea quenched our thirst. Kathleen and I had purchased gift bags with samples of makeup for each guest. My heart swelled with joy, gratitude, and pride because of the love that filled the air.

Between the hilarity and the stories we shared, we decided, "What happens in Rochester, stays in Rochester!"

A Modern Day Missionary

One luxury I maintained throughout hospitalizations and treatments was having my nails manicured. Jim chauffeured me to appointments and waited for me. The salon's environment was far outside his comfort zone. He was grateful for their free Wi-Fi so he could pass time with his iPhone. I liked the familiarity of the nail salon contrasted to the hospital.

I greeted the staff and Chhung directed me to a chair across from Linda. Many might be familiar with the stereotyped nail salons of various ethnic origins from Cambodian to Thai to Chinese to Malaysian. Linda (known to her family as My-lin) was Cambodian and had been my nail technician for the past twenty years. Whenever she was not available, one of her relatives took care of me.

My friend, Becky, drove me to one nail appointment. As we entered the salon, Linda's brother, Chhong, greeted me and asked me to be seated at his station. Another technician, whom I didn't know, came up with tears in her eyes and embraced me. She knew I had cancer, and she told me she had been praying for me. I thanked her for her prayers, but she remained inconsolable. In broken English, she informed us she had lost her sister, at forty-two, to stomach cancer the previous year. Her sister had lived in Malaysia with her husband and three little children.

This young employee cried with grief. She spoke to Becky and me of the risk she had taken in her home country, Malaysia, by becoming a Christian in a Muslim country. It had been an uphill battle within her own family to get them to accept the Christian message. She moved to Cambodia where the religion was Buddhism. She spent four years in Cambodia as a missionary teaching Christianity to small children.

When she stepped away, I asked Chhong to write her name on a card so I could remember. He wrote "E-Lin." It shocked me when he said that E-Lin was his wife. I never realized Chhong was Christian, and E-Lin appeared to be so young.

What a witness E-Lin was to spreading the Christian faith. Miracles happened around me.

Silver and Gold

Do you recall the campfire song with the phrase, "Make new friends, but keep the old, one is silver and the other gold?" I cherished my friendships, both old and new, as if they were precious jewels. My treasure chest of friends was better when shared.

Jim gave me a "Get Out of Jail Free" pass to go out with two girlfriends. I had been doing my exercises, napping, and nibbling at mealtime. He had stringent guidelines for me to follow. I did as he asked.

This lunch date became my first excursion without supervision from the home front. I took a bath, applied makeup, pulled on my wig, and dressed myself in preparation for the outing. I deemed myself pretty.

Cancer wreaked havoc on my self-image. I had lost fifteen pounds since my diagnosis, so few of my clothes fit. I would not recommend chemotherapy for weight loss. It was too expensive and made you nauseated. I was not sure if Jim would appreciate the side effect of a whole new wardrobe! I dressed in a pair of white slacks and a blue sweater set.

Betsy picked me up, and we met Sandy at Michael's Restaurant. Years earlier, the three of us had formed the "40 Club." Sandy and Betsy were two years older than me, so when I turned forty, they granted me membership to their club of two. Our children were close in age, and together we participated in the Catholic schools activities. It was such a delight to be with these two supportive friends as we caught up on news of grandchildren, travels, and part-time jobs.

This social engagement opened my eyes to the fact that I had become frozen in time. Betsy and Sandy were grandmothers but their grandchildren lived in town. We imparted stories about our toddler grandbabies. Each one thought that her grandchildren were the cutest and smartest. Garrison Keillor said Minnesotans are, "A land where all the women are strong, all the men are good looking, and the children are above average."

Sandy and her husband spent long weekends at a cabin up north so she described how much she enjoyed fishing and going into town for church on Sundays.

Both Sandy and Betsy worked part-time at Chico's, a clothing store for women. Their fashion taste was impeccable. They divulged details about the good deals at the store. I had been the queen of bargains when I worked at Herberger's.

They asked questions about my health and treatments, but they didn't dwell on my disease, as this was a happy occasion.

It compelled me to realize that everyone else's lives were moving forward. The laughter forced me to forget the battle that raged inside.

Betsy dropped me off at home just as the cell phone range. Jim wanted to know where I was. Seriously, I felt like Cinderella as I came in through the garage door, dropping my glass slipper as the clock struck 5:00! I hurried to the sofa in the family room, reveling in the fortune of girlfriends.

A Snapshot of our Lives

In February 2011, Jim and I drove to Kansas City for a wedding. It was a daughter of a life-long friend, Adella. I had started kindergarten with Adella and another friend, Anne, and the friendship continued through high school. Patty and Betsy joined our pack in high school. Our relationships have endured through time. After our kids grew up, we made it a point to travel together annually, and sometimes we included spouses. This wedding sufficed for our annual gathering.

Adella's daughter, Amy, was a petite bride adorned in an ornate gown that probably weighed more than Amy. The groom displayed a happy and joyful face. The sermon caught my attention to the point I wrote it down so I could share it with Kathleen. One key point was not to put value in things. Money can't buy happiness.

Jim and I discovered importance in friends over things early in our marriage. I reflected on those happy memories on our drive back to Rochester after the wedding. The man behind the steering wheel had always made me feel as the most important "thing" in his life. Jim and I married when he was in medical school, and we were on a tight budget, "Ramen Noodles and Hamburger Helper"-tight. We did laundry at our parents' homes.

In medical school and residency, we hosted parties with cheap wine and snacks. It was unheard of to go out to dinner, yet we were happy. There was no reason to keep up with the Joneses as we were all starting at a similar point.

Jim and I had intended to move home to the Kansas City area after he completed his residency at Mayo, but we realized in a short amount of time that the people of Rochester had become our surrogate family. Tim and John entered our family picture, and we became "townies."

We built the house where we still live. Residents, trainees and neighbors have come and gone, all leaving their mark on our lives through friendship. Kathleen came into our family when Tim was ten and John was almost eight. We started at the bottom of the ladder again when Kathleen entered St. Francis School when John was in eighth grade. I think we had one of the longest legacies there spanning twenty consecutive years. John and Kathleen followed Tim at Lourdes High School. We kept our faith practices alive by joining them in weekly Mass, the sacraments, and through service projects. Jim and I had deep seeded faith roots, and now they blossomed through our children.

Tim and John studied abroad during college. We joined Tim in Italy for Christmas because he was studying architecture in Rome. I imagine this experience heightened Kathleen's passion for Rome and Latin.

John was supposed to be studying in Ireland however the airlines delayed his flights as his departure coincided with the tragic event of September 11, 2001. He flew to Dublin ten days later. We spent Christmas in Ireland that year. Jim doesn't remember much of the legendary Irish countryside as he had to concentrate on driving on the left side of the narrow, winding roads.

Kathleen started college, and we became empty nesters. We thought we were living on Easy Street. I often travelled with Jim to his medical conferences and spent the time exploring a new city.

We acted in faith when we witnessed my parent's deaths, a friend's car-bike accident, the divorce of a friend, and illnesses of others. Jim and I leaned on each other during these tragic experiences. I reminisced that it was easier to give than to receive.

The tragedy of my brain cancer diagnosis stung me to the core. This diagnosis scared me. I cried in Jim's arms and he cried, too. We prayed to God. I heard God calling me closer to Him and sought to do His will.

Jim, my rock, encouraged me to fight the cancer, catered to my transportation needs, consulted with doctors, provided physical therapy, set up Command Central, dispensed medication with a spoonful of sugar, comforted me with prayer, managed the household and finances, adapted our bathroom, and protected me from well-meaning visitors. I drew on his strength and judgment during this crisis.

Jim has always been a dear. In 1997, my friend, Sandy and I were attending a Lourdes High School baseball game together. Our sons, John and Chris, played on the same team. Kathleen was nine and a regular fan in the bleachers. Jim stopped at the game after his workday at Mayo before heading to a night meeting. As he bent to kiss me goodbye, I said, "Goodbye, dear," while Sandy echoed, "Goodbye, dear." Those words appalled Kathleen. She said, "He's not YOUR dear, he's OUR dear!" Jim is a dear. He has that wonderful Irish wit. He is a man of faith and has blessed me since 1975.

CHAPTER 10

Round 2

Soul Time

On Monday, August 8, 2011, Jim and I sat on the sofa in Dr. Buckner's office on the eighth floor of the Gonda Building, one of many buildings that make up the Mayo Clinic complex. I was anxious about my platelet count because I had that pilgrimage to the Holy Land on the calendar for January 2012, and it was crucial for me to be healthy.

It wasn't long before Yvette, the nurse practitioner, and Dr. Buckner entered the room. Smiles on their faces offered relief.

The first thing I asked was, "Are my platelets high enough to start the next round of chemo?" The twenty-eight day cycle was important so I could finish chemo before the pilgrimage. If I heard a number greater than 100,000, I would be happy. I couldn't believe I was eager to begin another, often miserable, round of chemotherapy.

"And hello to you," they replied. Yvette and Dr. Buckner were beginning to understand my personality and what it meant to continue on with this chemo regime.

"Let's pull your records up on the computer." The computer ramped up slowly. Dr. Buckner turned and asked, "How did you do on your first round of chemo?"

"I was miserable, but Yvette answered my questions when I called her." I needed assurance that the side effects were normal.

As Dr. Buckner pulled up the latest blood tests, he informed me, "Your platelets are 121,000. You are good to go for round two."

I grinned, knowing my body could pull off the next cycle.

"How should I deal with excessive fatigue?" I asked.

"We can add a small dose of prednisone while you are on the five days of Temodar. That will give you energy when you need it." I appreciated the small amount of steroids to ease drowsiness.

"I am still having trouble sleeping through the night," I said. Would my normal sleep cycle ever return? After my biopsy, the doctors put me on high doses of steroids to reduce the brain swelling. Those pills kept me awake for most of the night.

"Would you like to try Ambien, a sleeping pill?"

"I'll try anything." I remember Dr. Buckner telling me I needed to get my rest during chemo, or I could provoke another seizure.

"How is the Miralax working for your constipation?"

"I need a prescription for a more powerful laxative."

Before you get the wrong idea, I didn't want to become dependent on prescription medicine, but I sought relief from what was ailing me.

"Okay. How is your strength and balance? Try the heel-to-toe exercise across the room."

I popped up and showed him how I mastered the sobriety test of walking heel-to-toe.

"Sometimes I drag my right foot when I am tired." Jim noticed this too, and he always had a firm grip on my elbow."

"What do you do then?"

"It is a signal I should rest. I have cramps in my right hand when I hold the newspaper. Is that something to be concerned about?" Upon reflection, I recognized the hand cramps as symptoms just before I would have a seizure.

"Your dose of Keppra should protect you from future seizures if you keep resting. Call us if you notice more significant changes."

Dr. Buckner performed a brief, routine, neurologic exam, which I passed. We left the office, picked up my prescription for Temodar, and exited the clinic.

If this second round of chemo acted like the previous round, I would nap during the day at Command Central while on the five-day medication. Call me Sleeping Beauty. I suited up with courage for a more tolerable and manageable round of chemo. It required energy to fight this ongoing cancer war, and I was developing the skills necessary to meet my opponent.

These periods of solitude and isolation during chemo gave me good soul time. It compelled me to slow down. It was as if I was gifted time for renewal. When I had had radiation, I experienced nature with fresh eyes in sunrises and sunsets, the colors of the flowers in the garden, the smell of fresh air, and the chatter of birds. This awareness continued through chemo, but I added another dimension.

I contemplated my changing interactions with family, friends, and members of the community. I envisioned myself being supported by these pillars of people through their kindness and prayers. Saints delivered meals and offered me rides. God's glory permeated everything. My reward was a swelling gift of gratitude. My spiritual nature blossomed under His care as I read books and articles written by other cancer patients. I understood things about how others' struggles were like mine.

I changed my habit of being on the go. It had always been difficult for me to be still. On family movie nights, I often got up to fold a load of laundry, pay bills, or do other chores. If I invited my family to watch a movie with me, they said, "Are you going to sit still or be up doing something else?"

I struggled with the feeling of losing control. I had been a person in charge of my life, and now I had to readjust that way of thinking. Deep within, I wanted to know I could conquer the cancer demon. It comforted me to experience God walking by my side.

Home Alone

With tears in my eyes, I waved as Kathleen pulled out of the driveway in early August 2011 to return for her final year of college at Madison. It had been wonderful to have her home with us over the summer. Kathleen oversaw my physical therapy five mornings a week. Before she left she presented me with a blue ribbon and a Certificate of Achievement acknowledging "my perseverance and positive attitude."

Kathleen had chauffeured me to doctor appointments and errands, cooked creative meals, and cleaned the house. It was not the summer Kathleen had imagined back in April, but things worked out well for all of us. We made memories over the past eight weeks, among them the Josh Groban concert, the day trip to hike to a site overlooking the Mississippi River, and the wonderful day of beauty she had hosted for my girlfriends.

Jim continued with his reduced calendar by taking Mondays off work. This showed his dedication to our relationship. He took me on little one-day field trips to discover the small towns in southeast Minnesota.

Instead of having "on-site handlers" during this round of chemo, I would have "on-call handlers." I would call selected neighbors and check in with them and tell them how I was doing during the day. So, for the first time since June 1st, I would have four days at home *alone!* I deemed myself confident in this freedom. Along with the independence, came new limitations I respected. I had to remain on the main floor. I was happy to have my laptop computer so I could write my CaringBridge entries or read devotional books. Did I see a glimmer of light at the end of this cancer tunnel?

My sister, Julie, posted a card that said, "Chemo sucks ... But if it sucks the cancer out of you then 'Yay chemo!'" I was glad that Hallmark created a line of cards that used jokes to help cancer patients keep a sense of humor.

Jim's sister, Pam, surprised me with a gift box containing chick-flick DVDs, snacks and bath products. I finally had the time to lie on the sofa and watch a movie and munch on the snacks.

My sister, Ann, mailed me The Bible on an MP3 player. As I listened to the Word of God, it imparted hope. I used the thoughtful gift during my sleepless nights as there were many of those.

My brother, John, sent me a book entitled *Jesus Lives* by Sarah Young. There was a passage where she discusses Jesus taking on brokenness. The passage states:

> *"Your weakness and brokenness draw Me ever so near you. You can open up to Me because I understand you perfectly. My compassion for you is overflowing. As you open up yourself to My healing Presence, I fill you with the peace that transcends understanding. So stop trying to figure everything out. Instead, lean on Me, letting your head rest on My chest. While you rest, I will be watching over you and all that concerns you. Trust Me in the depths of your being, where I live in union with you. My healing work in you is most effective with you actively trusting Me. This is the essence of My compassion for you: No matter how desperate your circumstances,*

the one thing you can always count on is My unfailing love."

Taken from *Jesus Lives* by Sarah Young Copyright © 2009. Used by permission of Thomas Nelson.

I felt compelled to surrender this cancer to the Lord and to trust in what He has planned for me. It was my faith that offered me peace.

Live Well

Balance in life was vital in case life took an unexpected turn. I had a talent for organizing and prioritizing in my home, work, parish, and our children's schools. Yes, my spices are alphabetized! Keeping relationships with family and friends were the key to this steadiness. I suppose that drive to balance was a reason I never stayed still.

I could never foresee a cancer diagnosis. In a recent issue of Mayo's *Live Well* magazine, Dr. Amit Sood stated that people need to cultivate resilience. Dr. Sood offered four parts to resilience that allowed people to cope and bounce back from adversity. These included: First, develop physical resilience. Eating healthy meals, exercising, and getting enough sleep fulfilled the first requirement. Friends delivered nourishing meals, Kathleen provided PT, and medication helped me sleep.

Second, use cognitive and mental resilience. Flexibility became an evolving characteristic as I realized not everything had to be set in stone. I had to learn to focus on the moment.

The third part of resilience was emotional. I didn't know my day-to-day fate, but I realized I had to adjust my outlook by asking if something was vital. I began to reprioritize my life.

The final aspect of resiliency involved spirituality. I acquired the ability to be still and let God come into my life. I acknowledged nature as a gift from the Master Artist. These traits become prominent in me because I had a firm faith foundation. God wanted a deeper relationship with me and this connection uplifted me. I worked to become the person He created me to be.

The Barber Shop

At my request, Jim purchased a pair of hair clippers so he could give me buzz cuts. A set of clippers cost less than a visit to the salon. I liked saving money any way possible. My hair had grown back in patches and my head resembled a chia pet. Jim lugged the metal stepstool up from the basement and we set up a beauty shop in the garage. He covered me with a towel after I settled on the throne. The clippers cobbled over my fuzz. We reflected on the times Jim had used clippers on our sons' hair between trips to the barbershop. Jim completed the chore in just minutes. When I scrutinized myself in the hand-held mirror, I looked like a lopsided cue ball since I had no hair at the biopsy site.

I gave Jim a peck on his cheek and went upstairs to shower while he shook out the fuzz in the towel over the grass. This became a monthly ritual for the next six months. I wore scarves and hats when I was home and saved the wig for when we went out. My appearance made me self-conscious since everyone knew I had cancer. I hoped to avoid pity.

Mother Nature's Beauty

On a whim, and because I had recovered from the nausea from the second round of chemo, Jim and I redeemed frequent flier miles. We flew to Kalispell, Montana, to explore Glacier National Park. This trip had top billing on our "Bucket List."

The term "Bucket List," coined after a movie by that name, involved a plot with two men who had terminal diagnoses. The men checked themselves out of the hospital to do the things they had always intended to do.

Jim and I had a bucket list of where we would like to travel. Jim's top destination had been to dive the Great Barrier Reef. He was able to scuba there in May 2010, and I went along to snorkel. The top of my list included the upcoming 2012 pilgrimage to the Holy Land. This vacation to Glacier National Park and a trip to the Great Smoky Mountains remained on our list.

Accommodations in the park were full, so we elected to stay at a resort outside Whitefish, Montana, and located 30 miles from the west entrance of the park. It straddled the Canadian border in the northwest corner of the state, a thousand miles west of Rochester.

Accommodations, visitor centers, and the shuttles all close on Labor Day, so we were glad to have made the trip in August.

Mother Nature's breathtaking landscape did not disappoint us. She displayed her late summer colors in the rugged mountains, steep valleys and lush green forest floor with a carpet of wild flowers. The aspen leaves had just started to turn golden. Their leaves waved to us as we rode by in a rental car on the narrow mountain roads. Tall evergreens stood at attention, marching up to the tree line in the mountains.

We spent four hours on the "Going-to-the-Sun-Road" because of the hairpin curves and steep inclines. There were plenty of turnouts for photo opportunities for amateur and professional photographers alike.

Glacier National Park offered a well-designed system of shuttles that transported visitors, at no charge, throughout the park. We used the shuttle as hop-on and hop-off transportation. That way, we saw the sights of various venues, such as mountain paths, open valleys, or rivers and lakes. This represented nature's finest art.

I acclimated to the altitude to do an easy hike. We hiked three miles every day on paths covered with pine needles, rocks, or exposed tree roots. The scent of pine filled the forest. We hoped to blaze a trail one day until a sign at the trailhead warned us that a mountain lion was in the area, so Jim and I hiked elsewhere.

All the trailheads had signs that warned of bear attacks. The visitor center encouraged hikers to make noise and carry a "bear bell" to scare them away. I have heard of cowbells, dumbbells, church bells, but never bear bells.

While we were driving in the park, we spotted a mother grizzly and her two cubs foraging for huckleberries on the mountain slope. I was unfamiliar with huckleberries, but they were popular in the visitor center gift shops. We watched a black bear by a mountain stream fishing for his dinner. A mountain goat stood on a massive rock near the side of the road as if he was on tourist duty.

The lakes were crystal clear and smooth as glass, with the mountain peaks reflected in the water. The noisy waterfalls flowed swiftly, ending in rivers ideal for fishing. Park rangers informed us the lake temperature was forty degrees, so we stayed out of the water.

We dressed in layers as the mornings were chilly. With temperatures around eighty degrees in the day, it made for perfect hiking. The blue skies, with occasional white puffy clouds, gave us an opportunity to play that child's game describing what you saw in the clouds. Animals, like an elephant with a trunk or a horse with its tail traded places with Dr. Seuss creatures in the sky. Our imaginations created funny images.

The lack of crowds surprised us. Employees said many schools had started classes.

We took a boat ride on the Swiftcurrent and Josephine lakes. I enjoyed the scenery as evergreens pointed their fingers skyward around the emerald lake. I dozed with the gentleness and rocking of the boat. My nap proved worthwhile when Jim and I finished a three-mile hike around the lake. This hiking increased my appetite, but we were careful not to share our picnic lunches with the critters in the park.

Besides hiking, Glacier National Park offered fishing, camping, biking, and horseback riding. Log cabins, along with a Swiss chalet lodge, offered tourists a place to gather, spend the night and dine. Colorful flowers spilled out of window boxes on these buildings. People of all ages and abilities loved to encounter the wonders of nature from the mountains to the valleys. The park offered a feast for the senses.

From a booklet called *God's Word for Today*, came a reflection that tied together my vacation. The premise of the reflection is:

> *"The mountains are a great place for physical exercise using well-worn trails. The path can be safe and scenic, and instead of watching every footfall, you can enjoy the freedom of looking at the view. So it goes when you habitually walk in the direction God has given you."*

Appreciate the view as you walk on the trail God has made for you.

CHAPTER 11

Round 3

Set Back

The changes the doctor suggested after round one of chemo rendered the second round more tolerable. I let the drugs do their work inside my body while I rested. Nausea plagued me, so to escape the queasiness, I slept under the twenty-star quilt Becky made for me. My phase in dreamland made the time pass faster. The steroids helped with my fatigue, and the Ambien allowed me to sleep a little better at night. The prescription laxative offered relief. By the third week of the cycle, I felt more or less normal. Optimism filled my spirit.

On August 31, 2011, I had blood tests and an MRI in the morning. The results would be ready at my afternoon appointment with Dr. Buckner. Since I had met my insurance deductible, my MRIs were free now. I searched for the silver lining in everything I encountered. Mentally, I was ready to begin round three of oral chemotherapy.

Jim and I waited for Yvette and Dr. Buckner to enter the exam room. The room had familiarity to us since this appointment was for starting my third round of chemo. We sat on the built-in sofa next to the built-in desk. Angled across from the sofa was an exam table. Office art hung on the walls.

My mind surged with expectations. The last two rounds of chemo went according to schedule. When I had first started chemo, Dr. Buckner told me that chemo blended art and science. He could not guarantee the pattern of five days on and twenty-three days off. The platelet count was key to continuing chemo. Because platelet cells are necessary for clotting, producing too few platelets put me at risk for bleeding.

Yvette and Dr. Buckner greeted us with warm smiles and handshakes, and hugs from Yvette. Something about their demeanor caused me to surmise my platelets were not high enough to start the third round on Labor Day. This would be a setback for me.

"Good afternoon," they both said.

"I hope you have had a pleasant summer," Dr. Buckner added.

"We have. It has gone so fast," I replied. The routine of cancer treatments and their challenges evolved to acceptance of the disease.

Dr. Buckner took a seat at the computer desk while Yvette sat in a chair in the corner. He offered me a look at the new MRI results. "The radiologist read your scan as stable, and I see subtle changes of improvement."

"I need a picture of that MRI on my phone," I said happily. I documented my saga with pictures and CaringBridge posts.

"How many platelets do I have?"

"Your platelet count is 93,000. They are too low to begin the third round on Monday," replied Dr. Buckner.

Disappointment clouded the discussion at that moment. Being a planner, the postponement in treatment did not mesh well with me. Jim reminded me the disease sets the schedule and I needed to surrender control. I left the clinic with a schedule for another blood draw the week after Labor Day.

We came home to Command Central, and I moped. I had been fighting this disease with fierce abandonment, but now I ruminated on why my body had betrayed me. My disappointment led me to look for answers in my devotional books. I returned to cultivating my seed of faith through prayer. God provided this time for me to grow in holiness. He called me into a deeper relationship with Him. I continued to strive to do His will.

I posted a CaringBridge entry asking readers for suggestions on how to raise my platelet count. Most people responded that I should eat liver. That would not happen! I hate liver. In reality, there was no way to increase the platelet count.

Because I had an extended break from chemo, Jim's brother, Bob, and his wife, Ellen, came for Labor Day weekend. They liked to golf, so I rode in the cart with Ellen. Ellen thought that my temporarily revoked driver's license included golf carts. Ellen kept her own score, although I should have tried to engage my brain by keeping her score. It was important to exercise my mind to prevent chemo brain when thoughts and words become muddled.

The next weekend, our medical school friends, Terry and Elaine, drove up from Lawrence, Kansas, the home of our alma mater, the mighty Jayhawks. We lingered over breakfast coffee at the kitchen table before heading to an apple orchard. Under a cloudless sky, we inhaled the scents of the fruits on the trees. We did a wine tour in southeast Minnesota in the afternoon before a freeze destroyed the grapes. I could not join in the wine tasting due to my medications, and I could not be the designated driver, but I had an appetite for cheese and crackers as the others tasted the wines.

We laughed and reminisced over the memories we shared. Jim and Elaine had been in the same German class at K.U. and Elaine was often late for class. The professor called on her, Fraulein Maher, to make a point of her tardiness.

Elaine and I were opposite personalities. When I first met Elaine, she was an elementary school teacher, but followed no lesson plans. The kids and parents adored Elaine as she made learning fun. Now she was a social worker in a Neonatal Intensive Care Unit in Kansas City. I imagined she excelled at her job with babies and families. Elaine was an advocate for the babies and parents.

Terry is a pediatrician in Lawrence, Kansas. He had a fun-loving nature, which suited his patients. It was like old times when Terry and Jim got together to exchange barbs. It kept the weekend filled with laughter.

We were Godparents to their oldest daughter while they were Godparents to our oldest son. Friendship therapy was the best.

After Elaine returned home, she sent me an email. It said, "I'm proposing the most powerful therapy on earth, 'Jesus assisted chemo.' These are my thoughts … as you know, we believe in the actual presence of Christ in the Eucharist. I was thinking … if you take the power of our Lord's actual presence and ask Him to personally deliver the chemo to the place it needs to go … what could be more powerful? Remember the hemorrhaging woman who touched Jesus as he walked through the crowds? She had the same idea, she believed his actual touch would heal her. I see this therapy working like that. Tell me what time you take chemo and I'll pray with you then." Elaine embodied true faith.

By mid-September, my blood tests showed my platelets had risen above 100,000. Alleluia! God knew what I wanted. He answered my prayers. I took Elaine's advice and called my friend, Betsy, to ask her to bring me Holy Communion during the third round of chemo.

I emailed my life-long friend, Terry, in September. She lived in Arizona. It was easier to pour out my heart and soul to people in an email who lived a distance from Rochester. I could be honest with how I felt. In Rochester, I reflected I had to put on a happy face.

The email stated, "I feel your support for me during this cancer journey. Sometimes I just want to give up and go be with mom and dad. Then I think how lonely Jim would be, and just as important, Kathleen. That is where I need God to help me with the word 'trust.' I used to think I controlled things, but that was not so. God blessed me with many things and made me think I was in control. I know differently now. Thank you for allowing me to be so open with you. God bless you."

Dining in the Garden of Eden

While on chemo, the doctor encouraged me to eat, and he didn't care if it had any nutritional value. My appetite varied from day-to-day. I wandered to my Garden of Eden, the kitchen, opened the refrigerator, and stared at the contents. Surely something would appeal to me. I had so much to choose from since friends still delivered meals. Jim shopped for milk, orange juice, and bananas at the Kwik Trip store. As with the two earlier rounds of chemo, Temodar forced all meal options to be shelved for five days.

It was harvest time, but the fruit from the trees and the vegetables from the ground didn't tempt me. I ate granola and yogurt, and when all else failed, I dined on Saltines. I rediscovered a cookie from my youth, Vienna Fingers, made by the Keebler Elves. Does the elf live in a tree in the Garden of Eden? These cookies bridged the eating gap while I was on chemo.

My brother, Chuck, and other siblings kept me stocked with Waiter Express gift cards. Waiter Express is a service in which selected Rochester restaurants participated. If I desired a certain cuisine, I could call the restaurant, place my order and it would be delivered. How nice was that!

Remodeling

At the appointment with my medical oncologist, Dr. Hammack, I asked Jim to wait in the lobby. I wanted to ask Dr. Hammack a question privately. I broke down in tears. "What does Jim know that I don't know? Why is he so eager to remodel our house to make it handicapped accessible?" My prognosis frightened me.

Dr. Hammack understood the conflicts that raged inside me. With compassion, she responded, "He is telling you everything he knows about your cancer. No one is hiding anything from you. Maybe remodeling will make your house easier to sell when that time comes."

Before this appointment, Jim suggested that we consider remodeling the main floor of our house to accommodate a master suite so I wouldn't have to climb stairs. I remained practical. He could not convince me to go to that expense and mess. He eventually changed tactics and suggested we redo the main floor half-bath to include a shower.

I retreated from the "woe is me" state. I consented to converting the half-bath on the main floor.

Jim and I always sought several bids when we wanted to have a project done around the house. We asked friends for recommendations. One bid for the half-bath conversion looked like a hospital bathroom with a porcelain sink hanging on the wall and the plumbing exposed. It included grab bars around and a bland white shower. I preferred something that looked homey, not institutional.

We settled on a clever bid from a contractor named Jon. An oversized pocket doorway allowed a wheelchair to get through. He proposed a vanity top with a sink, and a cabinet underneath that slid out on wheels. This offered wheelchair access to the sink if I ever needed it. He constructed the shower as a roll-in shower for handicapped individuals with both a hand-held and a stationery showerhead. Towel bars functioned as grab bars.

Jim and I used his Mondays off from work to go shopping for tile, paint, fixtures, and lights. Antique brass was not a choice any more. That was from 1983. We used the new brushed nickel furnishings. My girlfriend, Ann, chauffeured me around town to shop for towels and accessories. The tile and paint were in earth tones, so I brought home several sets of towels to match. To highlight the brushed nickel faucet and showerheads, I bought a Kleenex box cover, a soap dispenser, and a trash can in the same finish.

The workmen taped off the front door area and the kitchen with plastic sheeting to save dust from spreading. That was good in theory, but we discovered it had little overall effect. We covered the furniture on the main floor with old sheets. Part of me was learning to be flexible and not take control of a messy job. When they finished the project, I could clean up.

Jon was easy going, and his two foremen were excellent craftsmen. They pounded, hammered and cut with power saws while I snoozed at Command Central. The music resonated of a grade school band. The life size puzzle fit together at the hands of the plumbers, electricians, and tile people.

At the unveiling, I said to Jim, "Thank you. I like it. It looks updated. Now for the clean up!"

Have you heard of the term predustination? It is the practice of cleaning before the maid comes. Jim had hired a cleaning agency when the doctors diagnosed my cancer, and then Kathleen cleaned for us when she was home in June and July. Now, it gave me satisfaction to clean the dust away and see the updated bathroom. I added the living room, dining room, kitchen and family room to the cleaning list and would tackle those rooms when energy and time allowed. Instead of spring-cleaning, I did fall-cleaning. I transformed back to my old self.

An Example of Flexibility

Despite being in less than Olympic condition from round three of chemo, I accompanied Jim to a meeting in Jacksonville, Florida at the end of September. He thought a change of scenery and a few days of relaxation in the Florida sun would work wonders for me.

Honestly, I thought he just didn't want to leave me home alone.

Even though I lacked get-up-and-go, I tolerated the flight well. I always felt invigorated after a trip to a tropical destination.

How could a girl from Kansas have such a passion for a climate so different from the Midwest? I loved the palm trees, the vibrant color of late-summer flowers, and the smell of the ocean air as we drove to the hotel.

Rehab in Florida suited me. I read books by the pool while Jim attended meetings during the day. When the weather turned to rain in the afternoon, I went inside to nap.

On the two evenings in Jacksonville, we called friends who had moved there. We spent one night with Tom and Sue, our former next door neighbors. They were recent transfers from Rochester but had acclimated to the easy way of life that Florida allowed. Tom and Sue have traveled the globe, so we talked about their recent journeys. We exchanged news about our families. Jim and I appreciated dining on the patio at Pusser's with Tom and Sue because outdoor dining in Rochester had ended in early September.

The next evening, we met our friends, Roxie and Paul, for dinner. We had been friends since our early years at Mayo in Rochester. The four of us developed a love for sailing years ago. We took sailing lessons on Lake Minnetonka, in Minneapolis, during the summer of 1984. Jim and I spent several summers sailing with them on Lake Superior before they moved to Jacksonville in 1988. We had kept in touch over the years and now we caught up with news on our adult children. We planned a Caribbean sailing trip together for the spring 2012.

My therapy in the Sunshine State served its purpose. I deemed myself rested and restored for the flight home. On Friday afternoon, we arrived at the Jacksonville airport two hours early to return the rental car, pass through security, and get to our departure gate.

As the passengers gathered for the flight to Chicago, we saw thunderheads building in the distance. The clouds obscured the sun leaving a ribbon of gold to define the storm. Mother Nature did not want us to leave.

The gate agent announced, "For those traveling on Flight 7371 to Chicago today, the flight has been delayed until 5:15 due to the weather. Please stay in the gate area so we can board when the storm clears. Watch the monitors for updates."

Jim's cell phone alerted us to a text with the delay information. This was the first of many delays. We didn't dare leave the gate area in search of a meal. With each hour delay, we visited the snack shop to buy the little bags of pretzels, peanuts, or animal crackers. Those little two-ounce bags were expensive!

As the clock ticked, we realized we would not make our Chicago-Rochester connection. Jim called his brother, Bob. He lived in Chicago and Jim asked if we could spend the night at his house. Jim also asked Bob to arrange a taxi to take us to his home. We didn't know when we would get there.

The critical piece of the delay was the fact we had four tickets to the University of Wisconsin football game in Madison the next day. The blessing was Jim, in a moment of divine inspiration, had brought the tickets to the Wisconsin football with us to Florida. We planned to meet Jim's brother, Bob, and his wife, Ellen, at the game. Luck was with us.

At 8:30 p.m., our plane to Chicago departed. Exhaustion set in from the delays. I had no trouble napping on the flight.

When we landed at O'Hare, even from the runway, the airport looked deserted. We remained on the tarmac. It took an hour for a ground crew and gate agent to arrive and allow us to disembark. By the time we entered the terminal it was 10:30 p.m. There were no friendly American Airlines gate agents to help us with accommodations or transportation due to the missed connection. The airport was empty except for the janitorial crew.

We followed signs to ground transportation. Jim's brother, Bob, arranged a white stretch limo to whisk us to his address. We grinned as we climbed in and opened cold bottles of Aquafina. The driver appeared to be in another time zone.

The following morning, Ellen and Bob drove us to Madison where we picked up a rental car. We drove to Kathleen's apartment before the football game. Kathleen was in her final year at the University of Wisconsin so this would be our last chance to experience a football game there.

We met Corey, Kathleen's boyfriend. He was an attractive young man who taught fourth grade in Gurney, Illinois, an hour south of Madison. They had met over Labor Day weekend at a mutual friend's cabin.

Kathleen wanted us to have the "full game-day experience." I reached deep inside myself to be energized for this non-stop action. We missed the pre-game parties, but we still enjoyed the day. Camp Randall Stadium overflowed with a sea of red. There was a tradition called "the third quarter jump around" where the fans jump up and down in the stadium at the end of the third quarter. The Badgers beat South Dakota State, and the band played a post-game show called the "fifth quarter." The excited fans swept us up with the crowds as the Badger blood runs thick through many generations. Kathleen started her own branch as she provided Badger clothing to her nieces and nephew.

After the victory, we invited the gang, Ellen, Bob, and Corey, to celebrate Kathleen's birthday. We went to her favorite place for pizza, Greenbush. It was a noisy, basement restaurant, but we had fun being together. While we waited for our table, we fired questions at Corey about where he had gone to school, where he grew up, and what he was doing now. To his credit, he took the interrogation in stride and had a good sense of humor. Corey stood about a foot taller than Kathleen, but it was obvious he had stars in his eyes when he talked to her.

After dinner, Bob and Ellen and Corey drove home. Jim and I had rented a hotel room in Madison for the night, so we invited Kathleen to come to the hotel with us. We thought it would give us time to visit, but we ended up being too tired to talk.

On Sunday morning, we attended Mass and then headed out for breakfast. Jim and I did not linger in this college town too long because we had to beat the 4:00 rental car return in Rochester. On our drive west on I-90, we noted the foliage turning red and orange while corn dried on stalks in the fields. Cattle grazed on hillsides and in valleys. Gray clouds hung low in the sky making a vivid autumn scene.

We made it to the Hertz rental return with one minute to spare.

This became a lesson for me in flexibility. I could not control the weather or the airlines, but I accepted the challenge and moved on with the weekend. It would be one for the storybooks. We were fortunate that Jim had taken the football tickets with him. His moral is: "always travel with an extra pair of underwear."

Extra underwear or not, I was happy to be home again.

CHAPTER 12

Round 4

Red Flags

On October 5, 2011, I had a blood draw. My veins collapsed with so many needle sticks. I went through three levels of phlebotomists – the novice, the skilled employee, and the supervisor – before they got enough blood to check my platelets. Each person apologized as they attempted to get blood from me. I understood they had a job to do and couldn't blame them, but it became a painful hour-long ordeal. By this time, my nerves were raw, so I remained silent. If I opened my mouth to say something, I might have cried.

The bruising from the attempts to procure blood looked like tattoos, so I didn't need bracelets. I would have preferred other colors to the yellow, green, and purple.

The monthly appointments with Dr. Buckner and Yvette had become routine. As Jim and I sat in the exam room waiting for them to enter, we discussed the upcoming weekend. We planned to drive up to St. Paul on Saturday for the festivities before the Twin Cities Marathon. "If the children's race starts at 9 a.m., I'd suggest getting on the road around 7," I said.

"Do you know where we should park?"

"John emailed a map of the Capitol grounds. We can call him when we get parked and find out where they parked."

"What do you plan to wear? They're calling for clear skies and a high of 60," Jim said.

"I'll wear layers and jeans and grab a rain coat just in case. Remember how fickle Minnesota weather can be."

"Are we going to go to lunch after the race?" Jim asked. At that moment, there was a knock on the door.

Dr. Buckner and Yvette entered smiling, with friendly handshakes and hugs. I wondered how they kept such optimistic countenances with cancer patients. They always made me think I was special. They were part of my fan club.

"Mary, what do you have to report since we saw you last month?"

"My third round of chemo was much like the other two. Nausea is still my biggest complaint, despite the Zofran."

"Perhaps if you take the Temodar at night, it might help your feeling of being sick to the stomach during the day," Dr. Buckner suggested.

That made sense. "It never occurred to me to take the chemo at night. I will try that."

Dr. Buckner hesitated, "Your platelets are not high enough to start round four of chemo this week."

The red flags that rose in the morning at the blood bank, waved through the afternoon. I attempted not to look disheartened. Yvette and Dr. Buckner realized how important it was for me to finish chemo before Christmas so I could go on the pilgrimage to the Holy Land in January.

We left the doctor's office with an appointment for a blood draw the next week.

Jim and I drove to the Twin Cities on Saturday to see Reagan and Dylan "compete" in the children's day activities before the Twin Cities Marathon. The event took place on the grounds around the state capitol, under a cloudless sky. Hundreds of parents and children tromped over the freshly mowed grass. The kids' activities included levels from the Diaper Dash to the Toddler Trot to the half-mile run for the older children. Everyone won a medal. Medtronic sponsored the race, and dozens of booths surrounded the field to encourage wellness. There were ideas for wholesome eating, which emphasized the latest food pyramid with the base of fruits and vegetables. Another booth offered suggestions for exercise in ways that we had played growing up, like the hula-hoop, hopscotch, or playing on a swing set. The sponsors encouraged parents to be diligent about their children's bedtime.

After the busy morning, we walked to the nearby Great Waters Brewing Company for lunch. Reagan and Dylan chatted about their medals and prizes. After lunch, we strolled back to our cars on the deserted marathon grounds. Dylan was too tired to walk, so John carried him. Then we hugged everyone and drove home.

The leaves on the trees continued to change from the green of summer to the jewel-tones of autumn. Brilliant scarlet of the sumac bushes screamed, "Look at me!" As the foliage fell to the ground, it created a crunchy noise under your feet. The air became frosty and filled with hints of smoke from fires in the hearth or outside fire pits. Everyone welcomed fall.

It was apple picking and eating time. I always baked apple crisp and cooked applesauce in the fall. This year, I just bought those items from the grocery store. I used to make Minnesota hot dish, a hamburger and tater-tot casserole. I had no appetite for the covered dish. Pumpkins adorned our front porch, set to be carved for Halloween. We added another layer of clothing for daytime comfort and another blanket to the bed.

I liked this reading from Ecclesiastes 3:1-8 concerning the changes of time:

There is a time for everything, and a season for every activity under heaven:

> A time to be born and a time to die,
>
> A time to plant, a time to uproot,
>
> A time to kill, a time to heal,
>
> A time to tear down and a time to build
>
> A time to weep and a time to laugh,
>
> A time to mourn and a time to dance,
>
> A time to scatter stones and a time to gather them,
>
> A time to embrace and a time to refrain,
>
> A time to search and a time to give up,
>
> A time to keep and a time to throw away,
>
> A time to tear and a time to mend,
>
> A time to be silent and a time to speak,
>
> A time to love and a time to hate,
>
> A time for war and a time for peace

And In This Corner...

In my mind, I heard an announcer saying: "In this corner of the ring, wearing black, is the ugly CANCER! Tonight, he will fight MARY, who is wearing sapphire blue. Jim is in Mary's corner right now encouraging her. Let's give her some applause." Clapping and cheers arose from the crowd.

I never realized the parallels between the sport of boxing and chemotherapy. My knowledge of boxing originated from watching movies like *Rocky* or *Cinderella Man*. Both boxing and chemo involved fighting during intervals called rounds. In boxing, minutes defined the rounds, while in chemotherapy they used days to define a round. I was ready to start round four of chemo and braced for the side effects of nausea and fatigue. My goal was a knockout win. I wouldn't throw in the towel before I punched out my opponent's lights.

Green Light

By October 17, 2011, my platelets had doubled, so I had the green light to resume the fourth round of chemo. I would try a different regime for this round by following the doctor's suggestion, and take Temodar at night, to see if I could stay alert during the daytime.

Sometimes, I cried to release the fears that occurred inside my head. Crying cleared my thoughts and allowed me to see things through a positive lens. My heart swelled with gratitude when I realized I wasn't on a flight to Vancouver when I had the first seizure. I had good insurance to cover expensive medical procedures and medications. Mayo Clinic provided the world's best health care. People delivered meals, offered rides, planted flowers and hired a lawn service for us. There was no end to the gifts, cards and flowers that relatives and well-wishers sent me.

I relied on family and networks of people to get me through this ordeal, so I couldn't let down this cast of supporters. I hid my emotions when Jim denied certain household chores. Little tasks that normally seemed insignificant became exhausting or hazardous. That included changing the batteries in the smoke alarms. Do you realize how annoying it was to hear a chirping battery all day? I didn't dare bring a chair over and climb up and change it. That might be dangerous if I lost my balance, so I waited for Jim to replace the battery when he came home from work. Being sick did not suit my personality.

Jim kept me on a tight leash. I respected his concern for me and my safety, but the new house rules challenged me. The main floor became my boundaries. I was lucky to have the laundry on the main floor so I did that chore. Jim preferred I didn't go outside to rake the leaves since my balance wasn't what it had been.

When I was healthy, I rearranged furniture several times a year. It was boring to sit at Command Central and have the same furniture layout. With the change in seasons, I asked Jim, "Can you help me rearrange the furniture in the family room?"

"It will have to wait until Saturday. If you are bored, you might reorganize the pictures on the bookshelves or read your cards. That should take you most of the day," he said with a wink and a smile. "I don't think you'll get into trouble doing that task." He let me do small things to prove my capabilities.

The winter clothes hanging in the closet when I had the seizure in April were still in my closet. The problem was many of my clothes no longer fit because I had lost weight. I only had a couple pairs of jeans and some exercise slacks to wear. So I called up a girlfriend and asked her to drive me to the mall to find a new pair of slacks. I adjusted to my new slender body. Can a woman ever be too thin?

My diagnosis led to mood swings. First was the fear of death when I learned I had cancer. I worried about Jim and Kathleen. What would they do without me? If I lived, would I be a burden to them if I didn't eradicate this demon of cancer? Tim and John had families of their own so I wasn't as concerned about them.

Denial tested me. How could I have gotten cancer? I had always eaten right, aside from the carrot cake, and exercised. It seemed like a bolt out of the night sky when the doctors told me I had brain cancer. So much for healthy living.

Chemo-brain tried me. I was prone to utter off-hand comments. I couldn't be sure what I was saying. Difficulty finding words and engaging my memory were two prominent side effects from the medication.

The lack of control and freedom bothered me. I missed being in charge of my calendar, but cancer took over, and he had his own agenda. When I woke up every morning, I mulled over how I would face my body. I tried not to let my poor health define me.

I longed to work at the department store. Work enhanced my identity. Susan and fellow associates turned into friends over the twelve years I worked there in the Accessories Department. Even customers wormed their way into my life. I tried to show senior citizens extra care at check out because I hoped a clerk showed my parents the same respect when they were out shopping in Kansas City.

I was in the store one day when an elderly man approached me. He said, "I know you from our church. I had the same diagnosis you have, but I am ten years out." He vanished before I could engage him in conversation. The statement left me awe struck and filled with hope.

I questioned if my faith was sufficient to support me. The family room sofa turned into my haven. I read a variety of devotionals, the Bible, and books by other cancer patients that helped solidify my faith foundation.

The CaringBridge site allowed my life to become an open book and empowered me to write about my deeper connection with God. I had nothing to fear with God watching over me. Over the last six months, I learned to be silent and listen to His voice. That voice often came from the beauty of his creation and the changing seasons. My roots of faith brought new shoots of spiritual growth and gave me time to concentrate on what I valued most in life.

I focused on my relationship with Jim. He was my partner on this journey. While everyone asked how I was doing, I pondered if anyone ever thought of Jim and how he was handling this diagnosis. When I asked Jim how he was doing, he replied, "It is not about me."

Sometimes his evasiveness frustrated me because I really wanted to know what he was feeling.

Between cancer treatments, Jim escorted me to concerts, day trips, airplane trips, and we celebrated the seasons of life. Life moved on, so I followed.

Books

One book I studied was *Climbing the Mountain* by Anne, a lay apostle. I could tell it was my favorite by how many times I underlined a sentence or a paragraph. The author writes regarding the love of God, going through discouragement, and joy in service. I underlined "If we become ill while on this mountain we will be brought up as though we are on a ski lift." I liked that image.

Hope for the Journey through Cancer by Yvonne Ortega was another book that had multiple emphasized sentences. Yvonne starts each vignette with a scripture reading and concludes with a short prayer she had written. I highlighted the sentence, "This recovery time takes us on a journey of faith." It was so true.

For devotional reading, I studied *Jesus Lives* by Sarah Young. Her writings were about trusting in God, resting in Him, depending on Him, and many other reflections followed by short Bible passages. Her message was, "Will you trust in Jesus' unfailing love?"

I read *Have a Little Faith* by Mitch Albom. This book dealt with a Rabbi in New Jersey and a pastor in an inner-city church in Detroit. Both men wanted the author, Mr. Albom, to write their eulogy for their funeral. The Rabbi stressed ritual, tradition, and faith in his life. The pastor had grown up in a world of crime so he had to overcome obstacles in his life to triumph in his ministry aligned with God. These men were faithful servants of God.

I read the controversial novel, *The Shack* by Wm. Paul Young. It has an unlikely premise of God portrayed as a woman. The message of relationships captivated me. God drew me closer to Him, my spouse, extended family and supporters.

Having a Mary Heart in a Martha World by Joanna Weaver described me. I was a typical Martha, wanting everything in place when visitors come, while it pleased Mary to visit with the guests. To meet my friends' needs gave me pleasure. God has a place for both Marys and Marthas.

War and Peace

Louis Pasteur, a French chemist and microbiologist in the nineteenth century, developed a vaccine and pasteurization. I had read this children's book to my children multiple times. In the story, they revealed the discovery of the rabies vaccine.

A dog had bitten a small child. When the child became sick, the concerned family took the boy to Dr. Louis Pasteur. He treated the child with the vaccine. I remember the book's illustrations of soldiers marching through a needle to attack the rabies germs. The battle began, and the soldiers fought the cartoon enemy. A war waged in this young patient's body. It took a while, but the small boy got better.

I envisioned the battleground scene going on inside my brain this past week. Soldiers equipped with medication invaded my skull to fight the brain cancer enemy. They knew how to destroy the cancer cells while leaving the good cells alone.

I appreciated the advancements in medical science that Louis Pasteur and others started in the mid-1800s that continued to the newest research in the 21st century. What other discoveries might we expect during my lifetime? Will a cure for cancer be next?

CHAPTER 13

Round 5

A Gold Star on the Chemo Chart

Taking the chemotherapy drugs at night earned me a gold star on the chemo chart. It helped with both the fatigue and nausea. I swallowed the six pills for the fourth round of chemo with plenty of water. That meant I had to get up to go to the bathroom more than once a night. There were side effects either way. Dr. Buckner prescribed a low-dose steroid (is that an oxymoron) to give me just enough get-up-and-go to keep me awake during the day.

During the third and fourth week of the chemo month, I had energy to pursue a few extra interests. I looked forward to returning to the St. Vincent de Paul conference at our parish, Church of the Resurrection. I appreciated their prayerful support over the past months, and I was ready to resume active membership. As the fundraiser for our SVdP conference, I researched resources from our community. Herberger's (the store where I had worked) held a Community Day sale twice a year. Since it was November, the sale was just around the corner. The event involved not-for-profit organizations selling coupon books for $5 to the public. The organization selling the coupon books kept the $5 from each sale. It was a win-win for the charity as well as the store, with customers redeeming their coupons. We accomplished our goal of raising $1000 during our first year of participation.

St. Peregrine

As my treatments continued, I had a lingering question. Why do bad things happen to good people? I was not putting myself on a pedestal, but I wondered about my diagnosis. Life was a mystery.

I discovered books to read concerning the subject. When Job was in the midst of despair, he raised that question, too. The answer is two-fold. God's ways are so far above our ways we may not understand. Second, it is often observed that when something bad happens, a good thing follows.

Another answer to that subject was God gave us free will. God cannot impede the consequences of our free will. We must trust in the Lord. Invite God into your life and continue to build a relationship with Him.

In the Lord's Prayer, "Thy will be done" implies that you ask God to change your will to do His will. Prayer can do that. The change might mean adapting to the situation at hand. God uses suffering to transform us and draw us closer to Him. We need to remain hopeful.

St. Peregrine is the patron saint of cancer patients. My brother, A.J., sent me a St. Peregrine medal. I had to do an Internet search for this saint because I had never heard of him. He lived in Italy around 1300 in an area where they denounced the Papacy. Peregrine changed his allegiance toward the Papacy, and asked for forgiveness from the Prior General, Philip. He asked the Blessed Virgin to show him the way to heaven. Peregrine devoted himself to Mary in a priory in Siena.

At age sixty, Peregrine suffered from varicose veins that led to cancer of the right leg. The friars concluded that his leg should be amputated. Peregrine dragged himself before the crucifix where he became drowsy. He sensed Jesus descend from the cross and heal his leg. When the doctor arrived the following day, there was no sign of the cancer.

The news of this miracle spread quickly. In 1726, Pope Benedict XIII declared him a saint.

This is the prayer to St. Peregrine:

> *Dear St. Peregrine, I need your help. I*
> *feel so uncertain of my life right now.*
> *This serious illness makes me long for*
> *a sign of God's love. Help me imitate*
> *your enduring faith when you faced*
> *the challenge of cancer. Allow me to*
> *trust the Lord the way you did in this*
> *moment of distress. I want to be*
> *cured, but right now I ask God for the*
> *strength to bear the cross in my life. I*
> *seek the power to proclaim God's*
> *presence in my life despite the*
> *hardship, anguish, and fear I now*
> *experience. O glorious, St. Peregrine,*
> *be an inspiration to me and petitioner*
> *of these needed graces from our*
> *loving Father. Amen.*

Besides prayer, cancer patients can read poems written by other people who had cancer. My sister, Ann, mailed me a refrigerator magnet with this short poem:

What cancer cannot take from you: It cannot take away your faith, shatter your hope, lessen your love, destroy true friendship, invade the soul, or take away Eternal Life. It cannot conquer your spirit. I don't know the author of this reflection, but I read this poem daily and found comfort in these words.

Priorities

After reflecting on prayers and poems, cancer provided time to rearrange my priorities. Cancer changed my perspective on what was important in life. The disease affects everyone differently, and it transforms those around you, too. My parents instilled a strong Catholic foundation of prayers, rituals, and traditions when I was young. My spouse, Jim, guided me with medical issues and reminded me to rest in our shared faith. Our three children visited me as often as possible, and the grandchildren were the best tonic. I couldn't forget Easter Mass at Saint Marys with Dylan playing on my lap as I sat in the wheelchair. He took no notice of my limited physical abilities. Each of my six siblings took time out of their days to write something on the CaringBridge site, send me a card or surprise package, or call me. My brother, Joe, lived the farthest away, in Florida. He kept up with my health via text, email or phone calls. Jim's family kept tabs on me too. Our local friends were surrogate family and prayer warriors on my behalf. I sensed the support of strangers when I had appointments at the clinic or when I went to church. I found solace from the wonderful people in my life and in my relationships with them.

Improvement

On November 7th, I had an MRI appointment. My hope was that the images would show a shrinking tumor. A positive sign was that I had my blood drawn without incident. For once, there was no bruising. I considered that a sure sign of being better. Now if the platelet results and MRI scan could be as promising.

Later that day, Jim and I sat on the familiar sofa in an exam room used by Dr. Buckner. I was eager to see the pictures from the MRI and hear how many blood platelets I had.

I liked the doctor's southern manner and professional stature as he entered the room. "And how are you feeling today?" he asked.

Since I had no tattoos from needle sticks in my arms, I replied, "Great! I am excited to view the MRI images and learn if I have enough platelets to start round five of chemo."

While we waited for the computer to wake up, Dr. Buckner watched me. "How did it go for you when you took the Temodar at night?"

"Much better than taking it during the daytime."

"That's good news."

The pictures came up on the monitor. "I see improvement in the reduction in the size of the tumor. We can't give a specific answer since this area," pointing to the views, "might be the persistent swelling from the tumor."

That news brightened my spirit. The drugs were working. "What is my platelet count?"

"They were 114,000 today," the doctor said.

"Wow! That is way over the 100,000 that's needed for the next round of chemo!"

Dr. Buckner asked me to do simple neurologic exercises, which had become familiar. I finished a simple set.

"You can pick up your chemo prescription on your way home today. If taking the medicine before you go to bed worked better for you, then try that again."

As we left the office with a prescription in hand, I wore a smile on my face because I was nearing the end of treatments. I hoped round five would be as good as round four had been.

I had an appointment with my medical oncologist, Dr. Hammack, the following week. She would test me and tell me if I could resume driving. When I thought about driving again, I had mixed feelings. I wanted my freedom to come-and-go, yet there was a persistent doubt in my mind about those quick decisions you make when driving.

This next round of chemo could earn me another gold star on the chemo chart.

CHAPTER 14

Round 6

Crying Uncle

Lousy. That is how I characterized round five of chemo. I sailed through the first three days by taking the Temodar at night, but I hit a brick wall on days four and five. The constipation made life unbearable. I called Yvette, Dr. Buckner's nurse practitioner. She suggested more fiber and water in my diet.

In addition, I felt "out of sorts." The side effects compounded to a new low. They included mood swings, fatigue, taking multiple medications, lack of appetite, and sleeping troubles. I wanted this cancer to disappear. When I explained my irritable temperament to Yvette, she said she'd write me a prescription for an antidepressant, Zoloft, to improve and smooth the edges of my mood. There was one cycle of chemo left to finish. I did not earn a gold star on the chemo chart for November.

Just before Thanksgiving, I had an appointment with my medical oncologist, Dr. Julie Hammack, as she would test my mental status before I could drive again. "Hello," she said with a smile on her face as she reached to shake my hand and Jim's. I smiled and returned the greeting.

"How have you tolerated the treatments?"

I had learned to be honest with the doctors. They wouldn't know unless I told them. "Not so good," I replied. "I've had many side effects." I gave her my litany of ailments.

"Many patients suffer the same way you are. You just have one more cycle. Hang in there. You will be glad when the final round is behind you."

She asked me to sit up on the exam table. The doctor gave me the usual neurologic check-up with which I was familiar. I followed her finger with my eyes as she moved it around my head. She tested my reflexes. I walked heel-to-toe for her. Then she directed me to take a seat on the sofa next to her desk.

"Do you remember when you first came to see me?" she asked.

"Yes."

"We will administer those tests again today."

I hate tests, I thought. I feared I might make a fool of myself if she asked a question based on something historical.

"The first thing I want you to do is to draw a cube."

"That should be easy enough."

When I took the pencil in my hand, I realized I no longer knew how to draw a cube on a piece of paper. My lines careened in various directions. It resembled the art of a kindergartener. Dr. Hammack was matter-of-fact as she showed how to do the task. I shrugged my shoulders as I turned to Jim. When I saw how easy it was, I thought I had let him down. He smiled at me in return.

She continued, "Draw the face of a clock. Show three o'clock."

I was proud as a peacock when I completed that test successfully.

"Well done," the doctor said. Jim told me that often, brain cancer patients only see one side of the clock. A patient might put the numbers, one through twelve, all on one half of the clock face.

"Now, count backward from 100, subtracting 7 each time."

"100-7 is 93. 93-7 is 86. 86-7 is 79," I counted.

"Ok. I will say five words. We will have a short conversation, and I need you to repeat those five words. Ball, red, sky, pencil, and elephant."

I can't remember the short conversation, but I remember being able to recall four or five words that Dr. Hammack had said.

"Good job," said the doctor. "You passed your exams. I give you the green light to drive again."

"That's great news! It's like I am sixteen again."

We both chuckled, and I imagined being behind the steering wheel.

"How's the dosage of Keppra (the drug used to control seizures) working for you?" asked Dr. Hammack. "We could reduce the dose."

"I don't want to cut the dose just yet. I might use it as a crutch, but I am comfortable at the current amount of 3000 mg." The thought of another seizure scared me to death.

"Fine with me. We can decrease the prescription at the next appointment. You will always be on Keppra, but we can eventually get you down to a daily dose of 1500 mg."

A sense of jubilation filled my soul. I didn't drive home from that appointment since it was snowing. As Jim chauffeured me home, I told him, "I want to resume my exercise classes at the Dan Abraham Healthy Living Center."

"It will do you good to ease into your old routine," he replied. It had been eight months since this journey began.

Independence

The following morning, I drove myself to the mall. I had longed for this independence. Now, I had it again. Besides the freedom, there was this incredible sensation of glee. Of happiness. I fingered the metal of the key and the plastic of the key fob.

I whispered a prayer for a safe drive. The freshly plowed roads made for a splendid start to the day. As I opened the car door, I eased into the driver's seat. I hadn't sat in this seat since April 5th.

I went through my checklist:

Adjust the seat position. Check.

Buckle my seat belt. Check.

Adjust the rear view mirror. Check.

Insert the key. Check.

Put my foot on the brake. Check.

Turn on the engine. Check.

The engine roared to life and so did the radio. I turned it off; I didn't want any distractions. The instrument panel lit up like a cockpit of an airplane.

I pulled out of the garage, braking at the end of the driveway before pulling into the cul-de-sac. Now I understood how those "little old ladies" drive; I had become one myself.

Cautiously, I steered toward the mall. I didn't want to cause an accident if my reflexes were slow.

A handicap parking place in front of the mall lay open. That piece of cardboard hanging from the rear view mirror was a perk. I stepped out of the car and entered the shopping center without an escort.

The colorful storefront windows drew in the holiday shoppers. I let the crowd engulf me and joined in the fun. Christmas carols blared in my ears. A festive mood hung in the air, along with the aromas from the food court. Lights dangled from the ceilings and dazzled my senses. People charged ahead as if on a mission to get just the right gift at the right price. Other customers sauntered as if this was a novel experience for them. I ambled in and out of stores, admiring the Christmas goods. My eyes soaked in the array of hues while my fingers stroked the textures of the winter clothing. Retail was in my blood.

I ventured into Herberger's, where I'd once worked. Familiar associates greeted me and inquired how the chemo was going. I sensed I'd come home.

When Jim came in from work, I was in a chipper mood. "I feel like my former self again. I drove to the mall and saw the Christmas merchandise for sale."

"Did you buy anything?"

"No. It wasn't about buying. It was about the choice to drive myself there."

December and the I.O.U.

At dinner after my appointment with Dr. Hammack, Jim and I discussed my return to the Dan Abraham Healthy Living Center, the gym for Mayo employees. I had been doing strength and balance exercises at home since the hospital rehab. "Please be cautious when you go back to DAHLC," he said. "I understand you've been doing balance exercises here at home, but you should be careful and not over-do the work-outs."

I knew he had my best interest at heart, but I didn't want to live as if I was a China doll.

My first few weeks at the DAHLC, I did not resume classes. I opted to walk the track and do the balance and strength exercises. Everyone asked how I was doing. Being in public made my self-confidence soar.

I picked up pieces of my old calendar commitments. As my hair grew back, I made an appointment with Gayle, my hair stylist. The last time she'd seen me, back in June, she had shaved my head. Gayle was like a bartender; she engaged customers in the latest gossip or news.

My relationship with Gayle was one of friendship that had evolved over thirty years. We celebrated the highs and lows in each of our lives. Gayle had had breast cancer many years ago, and the disease did not slow her down with her clients.

In early December, Jim and I drove up to Plymouth to celebrate Lindsay and John's birthdays. Reagan and Dylan were eager to help their parents open the birthday gifts and blow out the candles on the cake.

I had spent the last three years commuting to Plymouth. I had provided Granny Care every Monday for Reagan and Dylan. There was a unique bond between us.

The next weekend, we attended a performance of Handel's *Messiah* with our good friends, Kathy and Tom. Handel wrote *Messiah* in the mid-18th century. His friend and librettist, Charles Jennens, wanted to create a scriptural anthology. He used both the Old Testament and New Testament for his text. The Hallelujah chorus is the most famous part of music from *Messiah*. I let the spiritual music pour over me. At the end of the performance, the audience gave the Rochester Symphony and Chorale a standing ovation for their rousing rendition of this masterpiece.

On December 12, I had an appointment for a blood draw to learn if I had enough platelets for the final round of chemo. My disposition darkened when I heard my platelets were not high enough. It's a good thing they make pencils with erasers because I'd already scheduled chemo on my calendar. The earliest they could test me again would be on December 16.

December 16 could not come fast enough for me. I drove myself to the Clinic at seven in the morning for a blood draw and came home. Yvette, the nurse practitioner, called me at nine and said, "Your platelets were only 97,000." The minimum count for starting chemo was 100,000.

"I'd be happy to write you an I.O.U. for the three thousand missing platelets."

Yvette replied, "I'll have to run that past Dr. Buckner." I almost heard the smirk in her voice.

I grew anxious waiting through the afternoon for the call from Yvette. At 5:20, I learned Dr. Buckner had accepted my I.O.U. Jim stopped at the pharmacy on his way home to pick up my last prescription for Temodar.

We had dinner plans that night with our cul-de-sac neighbors. Scott and Lisa hosted an annual Christmas dinner. Lisa was a gourmet cook, and her desserts were delicious. This year, she served individual Baked Alaska for dessert. Lisa had coordinated the rides I needed for radiation, so she had a special spot in my heart. My spirit soared with gratitude for these friends and neighbors who had been my prayer warriors since the nightmare began.

When we returned home from the dinner party, I swallowed my chemo cocktail and went to bed. I didn't care about the side effects. My concentration was on the finish line. I offered a prayer of thanksgiving for the medicine and the culmination of the ordeal.

We flew to Scottsdale, Arizona on December 24th. I wore a big grin plastered on my face. Passengers might have thought I was excited for Christmas. In reality, my mood skyrocketed because I had finished chemo.

Four generations of McCarthys attended the Christmas celebration. Bob and Ellen, Jim's brother and his wife, hosted us at their Arizona home. We attended a Christmas Eve Mass. I said prayers of thanksgiving for the miracle of making it through radiation and chemotherapy. Human nature was a marvel of God's creation and combined with science and prayer, was a testament to life on earth. I will always praise God for the gift of life while my focus remains on Eternal Life in heaven with God.

Our three grandchildren were the primary source of entertainment in Arizona. Santa found the children even though they weren't at their own houses. The trio was comfortable with the faces of relatives they seldom saw. They went up to aunts and uncles for help to unwrap their gifts. They liked to play "puppy." Reagan, Dylan, and Emma crawled around and panted like dogs. The threesome sprawled out on the floor to watch new DVDs. I'm sure the pictures we took will be their only memory because they were so young.

The Christmas decorations were different in the southwest. Outside, they decorated cacti. Ellen trimmed their Christmas tree with copper and turquoise ornaments, reflecting the desert tones. We shed our winter coats and enjoyed the Arizona sunshine. We feasted on the meals Ellen provided. My appetite returned in spades and I gorged myself on the calorie-dense food.

We bid farewell too soon, but we needed a few days to recuperate and pack for the Holy Land pilgrimage on January 5. I had an incredible cancer journey behind me and I was open for what lay ahead.

For Christmas, I wrote the following post to my CaringBridge site:

"I can never adequately thank each of you for your prayers and support over the last eight months. I know that God used you to help me do His will. You have been His light and the hope in this disease.

Mary McCarthy

My gift for you is a prayer I have written. As the Christ Child was born today, let us rejoice in our Savior's birth! He came to share in the fullness of his love and hope and joy.

Dear Heavenly Father: I entrust my family and friends to you

> *as they have been Prayer Warriors for me*
> *during my journey with brain cancer.*

> *Shower them with Your blessings. Direct*
> *forgiveness where it is needed.*

Guide them with Your wisdom in their daily challenges.

Teach them the art of thanksgiving for all Your blessings.

> *Help them to trust in Your ways. Awaken*
> *in them a desire to do Your will.*

> *Continue to enlighten their spirits with hope.*
> *Lift them up when their faith is down.*

Take them in Your arms and love them.

Show them the way to Eternal Life in paradise with You.

CHAPTER 15

Blessings and Going Forward

Sometimes life leads you on a detour. A fainting spell at home led to the diagnosis of an inoperable brain tumor. Nothing could have shocked me more.

Overnight, my life shattered. Crying didn't help.

I don't remember ambulance rides, the ICU, or much of the rehab stay in the hospital. I endured a brain biopsy, several hospitalizations, and thirty-three rounds of radiation and six months of chemotherapy. Blood tests and MRIs filled my calendar. I had a frequent punch card for MRIs. Buy three, get one free! They were still expensive, but I needed to keep a sense of humor during the ordeal. The entire medical staff had my best interest at heart as they assisted me in fighting this monster in my thick-headed skull.

I looked for ways to reevaluate what was important. It was difficult to let go of routines. Cancer treatments determined each day's agenda. Losing my driver's license interrupted my freedom. Medication and treatment side effects were my constant companions: nausea, fatigue, constipation, and insomnia.

My emotions flared and stopped me in my tracks. Denial came first. How could I get brain cancer? Seriously, I had always eaten right and exercised. So much for living a healthy lifestyle.

Then I got scared. I was afraid I would die. That fear still lingers in the recesses of my mind.

The chemo-brain and cognitive challenges exasperated me. I had never been the sharpest knife in the drawer, but I had a gift for managing time, finances, and projects. Sometimes I worried that I had lost those skills. I had to give myself time to recover before I tested those talents.

I received world-class medical care at the Mayo Clinic. Patients travel from around the globe to seek treatment at Mayo Clinic. Mayo is an integrated practice that coordinates care between highly trained medical staff, nurses, technicians, and therapists. I was lucky to live in Rochester, Minnesota.

I could not overlook the practical aspects of the diagnosis. My husband, Jim, and I met with our financial planner and attorney. It was essential that our legal documents were up-to-date.

Jim said he didn't want to look at the file I labeled FUNERAL. After the deaths of my parents, I had made a list of readings and music I wanted at my funeral. I showed it to him anyway.

My relationship with God grew deeper and more personal. I sought refuge in Him, leaned on Him, and asked for His support to do His will. I read spiritual books to help me discover my purpose. It was clear God walked on this journey with me, and many prayer warriors guided me along the path. I marveled at how God made the human body resilient to diseases through medications and treatments.

Jim rose to his responsibility both as a husband and a physician. I counted on him to interpret the medical jargon. He reduced his workload to eighty percent. He supervised my medicines and made sure I was safe in spite of balance issues. I contemplated designing a new line of shoes: New Balance! Jim's faith spilled over into my soul, so I reaped those rewards.

My children, siblings and Jim's family extended prayers on my behalf, along with surprise packages and cards that arrived in the mail. Friends offered prayers, transportation, meals, and visits. The CaringBridge site became a lifeline to keep family and friends informed of my latest treatment. Journaling empowered me as I told my story, and the readers replied with compassionate thoughts.

In the early morning as I watched the splendor of sunrises, I soaked in the beauty of nature. The sky displayed many hues in the pre-dawn hours. In the evening, there were stunning sunsets as the sun went to bed, and cast light up toward heaven. Most impressive was the golden edge cast by the sun on fair weather clouds. I listened to the birds throughout the day when they twittered and tweeted. If I knew how to tweet, I would have joined them in their conversation. The fragrance of summer flowers and freshly mowed grass drifted in my open windows. Mother Nature came to life in my back yard.

As my health returned, I relished being able to cook, clean, and do the laundry. When I could drive again, it restored my independence. I discovered it was possible to acquire new habits to do things and be flexible with changes in routine. Words of thanksgiving and gratitude were always on my lips.

During radiation and chemotherapy, I realized I was actively fighting the beast in my brain. Now I reached the difficult part: trust. I have to wait until February to discover if I had won the battle and render the tumor powerless.

The opportunity to go on the pilgrimage to the Holy Land on January 5, 2012 became reality and my reward. That was my goal before cancer entered the equation. Showers of blessings rained down on me while on the detour with cancer. I can never adequately thank everyone for their time, prayers, rides, and meals. Everyone played a role in my recovery. I realize God has a mission for me, and I hope to answer His call.

CHAPTER 16

A Holy Land Pilgrimage

January 6, 2012

I stepped off the plane at the Tel Aviv airport and paused.

"What's wrong?" Jim asked. "Let's go!"

I couldn't move. "We made it!" I grinned, and Jim returned the smile.

A pilgrimage to the Holy Land had been my focus since my cancer diagnosis last April.

By traveling to a sacred place, I hoped to find answers to deepen my faith. I intended to immerse myself in the spiritual, inspirational, and educational resources of the Holy Land. To see the customs and traditions that have persisted for over two thousand years would be my reward. I was excited to be an eyewitness as we journeyed to the sites where biblical stories had taken place.

Jim and I had always made our own airline reservations, lodging and tours, so this was a new experience. A travel agent, Bonnie, made arrangements for the trip, which included airline and hotel reservations, ground transportation by bus, hired guides and plans for each day's itinerary. Jim and I relaxed knowing someone else would deal with any travel issues. Jeff Cavins, the pilgrimage leader, was our common link with the other pilgrims. Each of us had taken his Bible classes in our parishes. Bonnie distributed name tags before departure so we could find our group of 145 other pilgrims after we landed. After the logistics of claiming our luggage and clearing customs, we found our fellow pilgrims. It was easy to strike up conversations with our new friends.

We arrived on a Friday, a holy day for Muslims, so they had closed their shops. Jewish people prepared for their Sabbath: sundown on Friday until sundown on Saturday. Jewish women hurried to market with reusable grocery bags before Jewish merchants closed their businesses. They adhered to kosher food laws, which meant meat must come from mammals that chew their cud and have cloven hooves. Fish must have fins or scales. Jews can't mix dairy with meat.

Sabbath rules were evident in our hotel. One that we noticed was a separate elevator for Jews to use on their Sabbath. They programmed the elevator to stop on every floor without pushing a button since pushing a button meant work. We learned if orthodox Jews wanted to watch television on the Sabbath, they had to turn on the TV before sunset on Friday and leave it on until dusk on Saturday.

Once we unpacked and freshened up in our hotel room, we joined other pilgrims and Israelis who sauntered on the promenade next to the beach that hugs the blue waters of the Mediterranean. Adrenalin kept me going. The nation looked to be health conscious. Individuals were biking, jogging, roller blading, or strolling arm-in-arm by the beach. In the coming days, we would see how my endurance held up after six rough rounds of chemo.

I heard many languages being spoken as we strolled and absorbed the beauty of Tel Aviv. Jews spoke Hebrew, Muslims spoke Arabic, and the native tongues of tourists dotted conversations everywhere. This cacophony of sights and sounds followed us throughout the pilgrimage.

The first night I feasted like royalty on a Mediterranean buffet of colorful fruits and vegetables, olives, dates, feta cheese, chicken, beef, and breads. It was a miracle to have my appetite back as

I indulged in a wide variety of delicious foods for my chemo-ravaged body.

January 7, 2012

After a jet-lagged night of fragmented sleep, we woke up, showered and went to breakfast. The breakfast impressed us as much as dinner the previous night. Fresh pastries, cheeses, breads, fruits, and a salad bar offered nourishing foods to start our day. Missing were bacon, ham and any meat products. Kosher food laws state that dairy and meat cannot be mixed at a meal.

Jim and I had packed a variety of clothing to cover all types of weather. We had worn jeans and vests on the plane and opted for Khaki pants and a light fleece for our travels today. Our heavier coats could be left on the bus if we needed them.

Our travel agent, Bonnie, divided the pilgrims into three groups. Each bus included a guide, a priest, and one of Jeff Cavins' associates. Jeff's associates were his wife, Emily, and our travel agent, Bonnie. Jim and I boarded the gold bus with an Israeli guide named Roni who had worked with Jeff for many years. Over the next eleven days, Roni would teach us about the Holy Land including the history, geography, archeology, and religions. He had a good sense of humor, too.

Father Mike Schmitz from Duluth, Minnesota, was the priest on our bus. His youthful appearance made everyone question his age. His smile and humor were infectious. On our way to the first stop, Fr. Mike said, "A pilgrimage is not a vacation, but a journey to God. Ask God how He wants to change you, and embrace the change."

The third member of the pilgrimage leadership team, either Emily or Bonnie, helped with Christian teachings and logistics of the travel. We were lucky to have Jeff as our primary guide on the gold bus.

We drove out of Tel Aviv, a modern city with high tech industry, and passed fields of vineyards, papaya, and cypress trees. Crops grew year round due to the mild climate.

Our first stop was Caesarea Maritima, a former port, built by Herod the Great in honor of Augustus Caesar. Here we began a pattern that became routine for every stop. Jeff provided a history of the area and discussed a Bible teaching to link the Old and the New Testaments. He wove biblical parables into its teaching.

Jeff taught in the ruins of a Roman amphitheater at Caesarea Maritima while the sun blazed overhead. He contrasted Herod, an earthly King, with Jesus, the King of heaven and earth. This set the stage for our pilgrimage.

After Jeff's presentation, Roni escorted us around the ruins and showed us where they held Paul as a prisoner before being sent to Rome to appear before Caesar. It made me think about how Paul had persecuted Christians in Jerusalem, and how he converted on the Road to Damascus.

We wandered through the hippodrome where chariots had raced and crowds filled the arena to spot their favorite charioteer. By 2012 standards, I imagined it wasn't pleasant to observe the fierceness of the competitions.

Roni pointed to the remnants of the well-preserved Roman aqueducts, which carried water from the hills down to the towns. This invention, along with the arch in buildings, became Rome's architectural trademarks. Although aqueducts were not being used here in Caesarea Maritima, some are still used in Rome today.

We climbed back on the bus and continued up the rocky countryside to Mt. Carmel, where we celebrated Mass in an outdoor grotto that overlooks the Jezreel valley and the plains of Armageddon. We could see Nazareth far across the lush, green valley. At Mass, Fr. Mike reminded us to ask Christ what He has planned for our lives.

I reflected on that question because it was one I asked before cancer attacked me. I had fixated on treatments and forgot to ask Christ what He had planned for me. It afforded me spiritual food to contemplate during this pilgrimage.

After Mass, we rode down to the "tel" containing the ruins of Megiddo. Roni explained, "A tel is a land structure where cities are built on top of each other. Megiddo was a famous tel because it controlled the trade route between the jagged hills and the sea." We spent several hours at that site where the Book of Revelations says the final battle between good and evil will take place.

Still on adrenaline, together with jet lag, our pilgrimage continued. That evening, under a full moon, we floated in a boat on the Sea of Galilee. Jeff told the well-known story of Peter getting out of the boat to walk to Jesus. When the wind blew up, Peter cried, "Lord, save me." Jesus raised up his hand and saved Peter. Jeff told us, "Listen for the voice of God in the stillness of your heart." We experienced the sea like the apostles. Thankfully, no pilgrims tried to get out of the boat.

Our accommodations for tonight were in a "kibbutz." Families that specialized in an industry for their living, this one being hospitality, operated this kibbutz. This complex of one-bedroom apartments stood on the southern shores of the Sea of Galilee. I visualized it being a popular place for tourists to escape the summer heat.

One hundred and forty-five famished pilgrims gathered in the dining hall that presented an assortment of multicolored and nutritious foods. We sat with people from our bus and exchanged stories about our faith, job, family, and hobbies. We had a lot in common with these pilgrims.

Since we had reservations for two nights at this kibbutz, we washed clothes in the bathroom sink before going to bed to allow time to dry. This was a cycle repeated during the pilgrimage because there was no way you could pack enough clothing for a two week trip.

January 8, 2012

We wore fleece and jeans today as we rode north through hills to Nazareth. Along the way, Roni educated us on the various crops that grow in the moderate climate. The valleys were full of barley and cotton, mango trees and date palm trees grew in the low plateaus, while livestock grazed on the rocky hillside.

We celebrated Sunday Mass at the Church of the Annunciation. The homily was about our "yes" to God and what He has called us to do. I meditated on my diagnosis and what God wanted me to do with illness. I couldn't come up with an answer because my brain was working overtime to process the new sites and stories.

The Church of the Annunciation housed the grotto site where the Angel Gabriel appeared to Mary. The cave stood preserved behind iron bars. I pictured the scene I my mind. An angel emerged to face a teenage Jewish girl. Was she gardening or praying? Did Gabriel's presence frighten her? The angel announced, "Hail, Mary, full of grace, the Lord is with thee."

I would have looked around and said, "Me?"

The angel continued, "Do not be afraid. You have found favor with God. You will give birth to a son, and you will name him Jesus. He will be the Son of God."

"How will this happen?" Mary replied, scared by the circumstances.

"The Holy Spirit will come over you and the power of the Most High will overshadow you."

"I am the servant of the Lord. Let it be done according to your word." She responded "yes," to being the Mother of God, which showed absolute trust.

After Mass, we ambled to the nearby excavation thought to be where St. Joseph had his workshop. It was possibly the home of Mary, Joseph, and Jesus, too. I envisioned Jesus playing in his dad's workshop in Nazareth. Maybe other children played with Jesus while Mary washed clothes or prepared a meal.

A short bus ride away was the town of Cana where Jesus performed his first miracle, changing the water into wine. Mary came to Jesus. "Son, do you want your friends to be embarrassed by running out of wine at their wedding feast?"

Jesus replied, "It's not my time." He told the servants, "Fill the stone water jars." The servants did what Jesus requested. "Now take it to the master of the banquet."

After the master had tasted the water made into wine, he called the groom aside and said, "Usually we serve the good wine first, but you have saved the best for now." Jesus showed His glory so his disciples would have faith in Him.

We peered into stone molds used to make the jars that held the water Jesus had made into wine. Jim and I renewed our wedding vows in this special location. Tears ran down my face as we said, "In sickness and in health." I considered it a blessing to have Jim by my side for thirty-six years, and good fortune to renew our vows at the wedding site where Jesus performed his first public miracle.

We departed Cana for Kfar Kedem, a few kilometers away. This would give us a better idea of life during the time of Jesus. When we arrived, it had the atmosphere of a tourist trap. The pilgrims donned Jewish garb over their clothes. In a large tent, we sat on a colorful wool carpet and devoured chicken in pita bread for lunch. After the meal, we learned how to milk a goat, make feta cheese and bake pita bread. It was hilarious to see pilgrims, still in their costumes, ride donkeys. I couldn't bring myself to join in because I didn't want people to think I was using donkey perfume! It gave me a chance to consider, "What would Jesus do," when it came to riding a donkey for fun?

I impressed myself by my endurance. Talk about history coming alive! My concentration focused on the vivid images and rich experiences. I napped on the bus as we made our way back to our kibbutz for dinner.

After dinner, a bonfire blazed on the beach by the Sea of Galilee. The moon rose and lit up the night sky. Fr. Mike heard confessions. I told Fr. Mike about my diagnosis. "I want to go where God leads me and trust Him. The side effects of the treatments tested me. Now comes the element of trust. The challenge for me is, I wonder whether radiation and the chemo drugs have worked."

Fr. Mike said, "God has something planned for you. Get up every day and ask for guidance to do His will. When the angel announced to Mary that she would be the Mother of God, he didn't give her the full story. She didn't know her Son would be born in a manger or the family's flight into Egypt. No one can know their life story but God."

I cried as I walked beside the seashore, but that conversation offered me hope.

January 9, 2012

The following morning we were getting better at sleeping through the night. The eight-hour time change upset our biological clocks. They forecasted rain, so we took raincoats with us. We traveled up the west side of the Sea of Galilee. The Hebrew road signs and the distances posted in kilometers challenged my math skills as I changed kilometers into miles.

As the bus climbed the hills, Roni pointed to the crops and said, "You will see fields of banana, peach, and mango trees." As we passed a cow pasture, he said, "Israeli cows produce large amounts of milk because as a cow is being milked, it is being fed, misted with water, and the farmers play classical music for them." Maybe being a cow isn't too bad.

Our destination was Capernaum. Jeff Cavins taught a lesson in the remnants of the synagogue where Jesus had taught and healed.

Jesus set up the headquarters of his ministry here and chose his first apostles: James, John, Peter, and Andrew. Jesus used parables when he taught in Capernaum that the Jewish people recognized in context to the period.

About fifty feet away from the synagogue stood a modern Franciscan church, built over the excavation of Peter's house. Jesus lived, healed and taught here. The glass floor in the church enabled us to view the large excavation of Peter's house under the center of the church.

We celebrated Mass in this Franciscan church. The sermon described, "Expectation is the killer of joy or experience or relationship. If the pilgrimage is not what you expected, don't be disappointed. It will take time to incorporate this experience into your daily lives. Set expectation aside and let God direct you. He changes you."

After Mass, Jim asked Fr. Mike to bless me. I welcomed the blessing because many healing miracles happened in Capernaum. The most notable miracle was the paralyzed man being lowered through the roof for Jesus to heal him. After what I had been through, that story offered a deeper and more personal inspiration.

We clambered back on the bus and moved to Tel Dan, the northern point of Israel. We bypassed orange trees and avocado fields. When it doesn't rain, they rely on irrigation since water can be a scarce commodity. A three-foot tall barbed wire fence marked the Syrian border to the north. We stepped off the bus in our raincoats and hiked for forty-five minutes through mud to reach Tel Dan. This was also the site of a Canaanite city where Abraham rescued his nephew, Lot. The archeological site dates back three thousand years to the era of Joshua. It boggled my consciousness to realize the history that existed in this country.

We trudged forty-five minutes back to the bus. The exercise felt good. We headed for Caesarea Philippi, north of the Sea of Galilee. This is where Jesus asked his disciples, "Who do you say I am?"

"You are the son of the living God," replied Simon Peter.

Jesus replied, "Blessed are you Simon, for this was not revealed to you by man, but by my Father in Heaven. Peter, upon this rock, I will build my church."

With this pilgrimage, puzzles of the Bible were coming together. So far, we had explored cities and towns around the Sea of Galilee; Nazareth, Cana, and Capernaum. Each of these locations played a role in the story of the Bible.

Three busloads of hungry pilgrims descended on a restaurant that specializes in "Peter's Fish." Jim chose the fish while I enjoyed a pita stuffed with vegetables. Jim said, "The fish was bony." I believed I made a wiser choice for lunch.

The final stop of the day was at Tabgha – site of the miracle of the multiplication of the five loaves and two fish. A fifth-century mosaic on the floor depicted a basket of bread between two fish. I bought a clay-pottery bowl that replicates the mosaic and planned to serve hummus in it when I got home. This was our first experience with currency exchange. Israel used the shekel, but they accepted the U.S. dollar. Up to this point, there had been little occasion to shop, which made Jim happy.

January 10, 2012

The secret for comfortable travel was to dress in layers. I required more layers at the start of the day. After a hearty breakfast, we journeyed by bus to the northern coast of the Sea of Galilee, to the Church of St. Peter's Primacy. Jesus called the fishermen from this area as His apostles. I contemplated, "These men made their livelihood by fishing. How did they know to give up fishing and trust in this unknown person? Why would anyone follow someone preaching in a radical way?"

We had Mass in the courtyard of the Church of St. Peter's Primacy. As the priest said the outdoor Mass, we looked to the sea as a fishing boat passed by with fishermen pulling in their nets. A drop-off in the water there made for good fishing. It existed since the time of Christ. I visualized the apostles as fishermen, lowering and raising their nets.

At Mass, Father said, "Listen to how God will move you. There is no place like home. Home is family. Families who are in relationship with God should be the center of the relationship." I knew I kept God at the center of my life, but I worried about others who didn't make God important in their lives.

We left the seashore and rode a short distance up the hill to the Church of the Beatitudes. Many bushes and flowers were in bloom. It would be many months before I would see color, other than white, in Minnesota. I was a tad envious.

The church's location boasted a panoramic spectacle over lush green hillsides to the majestic azure of the Sea of Galilee. I wanted to spend all day here. The octagonal church capped with a massive dome, represents the Eight Beatitudes, the New Law.

The Eight Beatitudes are:

> *Blessed are the poor in spirit, for theirs is the kingdom of God.*
>
> *Blessed are those who mourn, for they will be comforted.*
>
> *Blessed are the meek, for they will inherit the earth.*
>
> *Blessed are those who hunger and thirst for justice, for they will be filled.*
>
> *Blessed are the merciful, for they will receive mercy.*
>
> *Blessed are the pure in heart, for they will see God.*

*Blessed are the peacemakers, for they will be
called children of God.*

*Blessed are those who persecute for justice's
sake, for theirs is the kingdom of God.*

We had an hour to reflect at this tranquil spot. I imagined
Jesus teaching the crowds in this natural amphitheater. Would I have
stayed in the crowd and been able to comprehend Jesus's teachings?
He was a radical preacher. Honestly, I doubt I would have remained
if I had grown up with Jewish traditions and customs, because I often
don't like change.

I felt relaxed, making it difficult to leave this lovely setting.
Jim and I ate a snack on the bus ride as we moved to our next stop, Beit
Shean. On the way, Roni explained, "The Sea of Galilee is receding
because there is less snow in the mountains, less rain, and more
people are using water. Israel is researching ways to get and use water
more efficiently."

We continued the drive alongside the Jordan River, the
lifeblood of Israel. This river was also the border between Israel and
the peaceful country of Jordan, but it was alarming to notice the
warning signs on the fence for land mines in Jordan. I sensed the
impacts of the politics, history, geography, religion, and cultures. I
thought of the comforts and security we take for granted in America.

We reached Beit Shean, a Roman city that was an archeological
site. Even ruins remained to picture the thriving city at the time of
Christ. The city was important because of its location on the trade
route between Mesopotamia and the Mediterranean. Cleopatra had
been here! I recalled Elizabeth Taylor starring as Cleopatra in the epic
movie because I like to watch classic movies.

Beit Shean prompted me to recall my visit to the Roman
Forum in Rome, which I had seen in 1999. Both locations had
remnants of columns and buildings. Faded mosaics remained on
some of the floors in Beit Shean. Jim took a picture of me in front of
what could have been the original Talbots! After the tour, we dined

on the patio overlooking the ruins. I wished there was a way for time travel, so I could see how people lived two thousand years ago. But the remains of this city certainly allowed us to imagine what time might have been like then.

We proceeded on the bus to our next destination, the Dead Sea. The topography changed to desert as we moved south. Although not a desert, I remember driving across the Badlands in South Dakota and it had a similar terrain. The Dead Sea is the lowest place on earth at thirteen hundred feet below sea level. It is thirty-six percent salt, so only microbial life exists. The sea contain an important mineral, magnesium, which Israelis extract and export.

We reached our hotel before sunset and Jim changed into his swim trunks to experience floating in the Dead Sea. I declined Jim's invitation to join him because he said the water was cold. Jim said it produced a strange sensation because he was buoyant, and when he returned to shore, a slimy coating covered his skin. People revere the healing qualities of the Dead Sea Salts.

Many people played in the indoor pool after dinner, but I needed rest to keep up the pace of the pilgrimage.

January 11, 2012

From the balcony of our hotel room, we saw the morning sun rise over the Dead Sea. The landscape of clay, rock and sand looked bleak. We dressed in long sleeves and khakis. We traveled north by bus to Masada, the wilderness palace on a high plateau built by Herod the Great. At ground level, we climbed into a cable car that carried us to the summit of this mountain. We explored what little remained of the buildings, mere foundations in the sand.

The citadel, built as a refuge from the Jews, later became a base for the Jews after the fall of Jerusalem. They occupied the site and used it as a headquarters for the last resistance against Rome in 73 AD. A group of 1000 men, women, and children committed suicide rather than succumb to Roman rule; that was the last time Israel owned land until the 1940s. I found this highland to be an incredible work of engineering. Roni told us that Masada was a popular tourist stop and, after seeing it, I could understand why.

When we departed Masada, a sudden sand storm whipped up in the desert, which was not uncommon given the dry ground. It was like fog, but instead of a cloud, sand in the atmosphere cut down on the visibility. I was in high regard of our bus driver's abilities to navigate us to the next location.

Our next stop was En Gedi – a nature reserve – an oasis in the Judean desert. Ibex and wild sheep roamed free. Many pilgrims had never encountered an ibex, a wild goat, so people took pictures of this new animal that appeared unfazed by humans. Biblical historians believe that David hid from Saul in the caves here and David may have written the Psalms at this setting. It amazed me that the events in the Bible had taken place at this place where our group was now standing.

Fr. Mike gave a short lecture. "Use the Psalms as a soundtrack of your life." He read the familiar Psalm 23. *"The Lord is my shepherd. There is nothing I shall want. He makes me lie down in green pastures. He leads me to still waters and restores my soul. He leads me in the right path for his name's sake."* He concluded, "Trust God even if you are asked to make changes."

For as long as I can remember, I have always wanted to be in control of my life. With the cancer diagnosis of last April, I had to give up handling all my household responsibilities. I had formerly prided myself on those accomplishments: finances, cleaning, laundry, ironing, and running errands were my fulfillment. Workouts at the gym, volunteering, social outings, and trips with Jim packed my calendar. For so many years, I felt I had given Jim the ability to work so hard and practice medicine without worrying about who was taking care of the responsibilities at home. It was hard to move aside as the queen of the castle and allow Jim to take over as the king. I wasn't giving up, merely stepping away until good health returned.

After we left the nature preserve, the bus driver drove us past acres of date palm trees. Sheep and goats grazed in the rocky yet tranquil terrain. We arrived at a military zone at Quasar El Yahud, on the Jordanian border. Several major events took place here: John the Baptist baptized Christ in the Jordan River, Joshua led Israel to the Promised Land, and a chariot took Elijah to heaven. After Jesus's baptism, God said, "This is my beloved Son in whom I am well pleased." Jesus, son of a carpenter, started his public ministry here. At this historical biblical location, Jesus stepped forward and revealed His role in salvation history.

I imagined the Jordan wasn't a muddy river during the era of Christ. It might have been clean water that could be used for bathing or washing clothes. Today, the brown, swollen river flowed swiftly. Our group of pilgrims celebrated Mass on a patio next to the river. The priest focused on the sermon. "Baptism is a new beginning. It has brought us into the family of God. The family is united in Christ with the bonds established with others. Faith brings order to our life and unites us." Family had always been my top priority in life. I received more joy out of giving to family and friends rather than receiving.

Jim dipped his hands in the Jordan River and we blessed each other. It was a blessing to share our faith, and it led me to admire my devoted husband even more deeply.

We resumed our journey up to Jerusalem and stopped at Qumran, where a Bedouin shepherd discovered the Dead Sea scrolls in a cave in 1947. At one time, a sect of Jews, called the Essenes, led a communal life in the Desert Mountains. They recorded the first five books of Moses, the Psalms, and Isaiah, as they had heard them. The text of the scrolls was essentially the same as the Hebrew text that many generations had learned. The Essenes hid these scrolls, written on parchment, in terra cotta jars in the caves of Qumran because if the Romans found them, they would be burned.

We wondered why the shepherd had come to this cave looking for his lost goat. Didn't he know this land was barren? It was rather comical to see caves at Qumran without food for grazing animals. Perhaps the shepherd, like Jesus, searched for his lost goat or lamb.

We boarded the bus for the ride up to Jerusalem on Jericho Road. Jesus would have taken a similar route from the Jordan River, through Jericho, and up to Jerusalem. Anyone who goes to Jerusalem travels upwards to the city. Figuratively, going up means going to heaven. That was my goal in life: to enter heaven.

At dusk we paused at Mt. Scopus, which offered a panoramic view of Jerusalem lit up with the city lights. Despite the chilly rain, we stepped off the bus to honor a tradition. We sipped a small cup of wine and said a blessing as Jesus would have done. It had been a long day of sightseeing, but worth every exhausting minute to experience sites where the Bible stories had occurred.

After we checked into the Olive Tree Hotel, I was ready for dinner. The buffet meals offered a variety of healthy options. We enjoyed our conversation with our new friends as we reviewed our day's itinerary.

January 12, 2012

I packed layers to wear on days when it was cold. Chilly air greeted us today. Our band of pilgrims walked the Palm Sunday route, simulating the way Jesus had entered the eastern side of Jerusalem before His Passion. We started at the top of the Mount of Olives, with a commanding view of the Kidron Valley. We knelt and placed our hands on the stone at the Mosque of the Ascension, the place where Christ ascended into heaven. I looked up toward heaven and prayed I would get there sometime. The anticipation of entering the Kingdom of God permeated my thoughts.

As we descended on the road from the Mount of Olives, Jeff Cavins lectured on redemptive suffering. "You can offer up your physical or mental anguish for the redemption of others. In suffering, we take part in redemption. One must unite their own self with the will of God. Suffering requires action. God will not allow something to happen that we can't handle. Keep an eternal perspective."

When I was young and complained to my mom about something, she said, "Offer it up." I finally understood her statement. My parents lived the Catholic faith by their actions and examples. I never overheard them speak unkindly of another person, we took part in the sacraments, and my mom could always accommodate a last minute visitor for dinner. I've strived to follow their examples.

At the base of the Mount of Olives was the Garden of Gethsemane. Gethsemane means "oil press," and the garden was full of olive trees, some of which dated back to the period of Christ.

Fr. Mike offered Mass at the Church of All Nations in the Garden of Gethsemane. A large, flat stone sat in front of the altar. This was where Jesus spent the night in agony in the garden, praying, before his betrayal.

The homily at Mass resumed the theme of suffering. "Jesus gives meaning to our suffering. Jesus lets us suffer so we will know his love for us. In our suffering, we can apply redemption to those in need. Redemptive suffering can bring joy." Further, Fr. Mike said, "It is a tragedy to not try to become a saint. How do you become a saint? Begin by praying. Enter into conversations with God. Follow Jesus to God and say, 'Thy will be done.'"

"Thy will be done" had been my mantra during radiation and chemo. I prayed those words each time I slid into the MRI machine and went under radiation. It comforted me to call on the Lord. Yes, there was suffering during my cancer treatments, but if it brought me closer in my relationship with God, that was my reward.

After Mass, Jim and I both knelt to touch the stone in front of the altar. I felt miserable when I contemplated Christ's actions to save us. Was I worthy of salvation? Panic seized me as I tried to tie my diagnosis to redemption. What did God want me to do with my diagnosis? Should I pray for a miracle? If I prayed for a miracle, would that be selfish? How much time did I have? I kept my attention on God and hoped he would answer my questions.

We left the church and crossed the Kidron Valley by bus to Mt. Zion, in the southwest section of the Old City. We entered a building and climbed the stairs to a room believed to be the location of the Upper Room. It was the site of the Last Supper where Jesus gathered his apostles for the Passover meal. He took bread, blessed it and said, "This is my body."

After dinner, Jesus took wine, blessed it and said, "Take and drink, for this is my blood. Do this in memory of me." Jesus instructed his apostles to do the same.

The Eucharist is the source and summit of our Catholic faith. The mystery of Holy Communion grows out of faith and is the new covenant. My faith has always centered on the Eucharist. My parents instilled in me the depth and dimension of Holy Communion. I never questioned the communion wafer being less than the Body of Christ.

Mr. Cavins pointed to a sculpture in the room of the Last Supper, the Tree of Life in the Garden of Eden. "With the Last Supper and the Eucharist, His death and resurrection allow us back into the garden. We partake in the Tree of Life by the Eucharist."

We left the Upper Room and spent the afternoon at a large, outdoor model of the first century Old City in Jerusalem. Roni introduced the historic information for our upcoming tour in the Old City.

We returned to the hotel for an early dinner because the travel agent had scheduled a private tour of the Kotel Tunnel that night. The tunnel runs under the Western Wailing Wall of the Temple Mount. During the Roman period in Jerusalem, King Herod expanded the Temple Mount by fortifying the base. When the Second Temple fell, the foundation remained. Charles Wilson and Charles Warren, British archeologists, uncovered part of the tunnel in the 1860s before they abandoned the project. After the Six Day War in 1967, Jewish people took up the excavation below the Western Wailing Wall and the tunnel can now be seen by tourists.

Jim had to wear a kippah, a Jewish skull cap, for the tunnel tour. He entered the tunnel through the men's door while I entered through the women's door, but we came together in the tunnel. We touched the limestone walls that support the temple and saw a glimpse of history while Roni educated us about the tunnel. No one knows if the Ark of the Covenant is buried in these walls! Wouldn't finding the Ark make a great movie?

January 13, 2012

Today we opted to leave our sack of laundry at the front desk to be laundered and returned to us when we came back later in the day. We thought the $15 fee was money well spent. It sure beat doing laundry in the bathroom sink.

In spite of the gray rainy Friday, I was excited because we were going to Bethlehem, the birthplace of Jesus. The town was five miles from Jerusalem, and seventy miles south of Nazareth. Bethlehem means "house of bread" in Hebrew. In Arabic, it means "house of flesh." Jesus offered His body as the bread of life. It seemed proper for Jesus to be born in a feeding trough in Bethlehem.

I hadn't realized that Bethlehem was in a Palestinian-controlled zone. A thirty-foot-high wall surrounded Bethlehem to thwart Arabs from escaping or terrorists entering. It reminded me of the Berlin Wall that divided the city of Berlin, which I had seen in 1981. Jewish people cannot enter through the guarded gate, so Roni exited the bus and a Palestinian guide took Roni's place. The Palestinian guide was not as fun as Roni. He recited the facts he learned in "How to be a travel guide in Bethlehem" class. I felt sorry for him as I suspected this was the best job he could find.

As we drove through the gate, the somber mood of the bleak city became evident. The unemployment rate was at fifty percent in Bethlehem, and many shops had gone out of business. The tourist industry had not kept the stores open. It shocked me with the contrast between what I envisioned Bethlehem to look like and the way it actually looked. I didn't like what I saw. I wanted it to be like images on Christmas cards or nativity sets.

What I observed was a deserted town with little hustle and bustle. The rain and gray skies kept me from a clear view. There was no festive atmosphere to celebrate the place of Christ's birth. I thought of how, in the U.S., we maintain historical landmarks. I glanced around for people attired in period clothing, vendors selling souvenirs, food peddlers calling to tourists to taste their delicious specialties, and guides who'd offer tours for a fee. None of that existed in Bethlehem.

Our bus let us off at the Church of the Nativity. The Greek Orthodox décor, with its many hanging candles, made the church seem cluttered. Seeing the birthplace of Christ was my focus, so I didn't pay attention to the guide as he explained the fourth century mosaics on the floor.

Jim and I waited in a slow-moving line to go downstairs under the church, to see and touch the location where Mary gave birth. When we reached the lower level, a silver star in a marble floor marked the spot. The fourteen-point star represented the fourteen generations since Abraham. Jim and I knelt at the spot to pay homage to our King. I reflected on a young Mary giving birth in a stable, surrounded by animals. God the Father provided strength for this Holy Family.

Father proclaimed in the homily at Mass, "God promised a Messiah who would bring us salvation. God put his plan into action with the birth of Jesus. Now we must put our words into action and allow the Holy Spirit to work through us. We need to trust in God's plan. God gives us a sense of hope."

Christmas will never be the same for me after the encounter at Christ's birthplace.

We visited the Shepherd's Field where the angels heralded Christ's birth. The caves in the field provided little shelter from the cold rainy day. How did the shepherds acclimate to the weather? It would be difficult for me to sacrifice the comforts of a cozy home and warm-weather clothing.

For lunch, we dined at an Arabic restaurant near the caves. After the hearty meal, pilgrims danced to Arabic music in this barn-sized restaurant. They swayed to new music; I chose not to participate because I have no rhythm.

We left the restaurant and went to a Christian store in Bethlehem. Olivewood souvenirs were one of Bethlehem's notable collectibles. Our guides told us the shop was only open for us. The shop owner locked us in the store for our safety! There was always a chance of terrorism. It was a sobering fact to realize people in the world live with that threat every day.

I wanted to buy a token for the long list of people who had been supportive of me while I had my therapies. The trip to the Holy Land had been my goal throughout the treatments. Bringing something home with me would show my affection for each person. I had fun picking out the gifts, and Jim assured me we had room in our luggage for the haul.

We returned via bus to our hotel, where we dined on a delicious Mediterranean supper, and enjoyed camaraderie with our companions before going to bed. We picked up our clean laundry at the desk before going to our room. It was a luxury to have clean clothes to last the rest of the pilgrimage.

January 14, 2012

Today required heavy coats, hats, and gloves because it was so cold. We walked to the Old City of Jerusalem and went through the Lion's Gate. I thought I had stepped into C.S. Lewis' wardrobe and came out on the other side. Instead of Narnia, I stepped into Jerusalem two thousand years ago!

Jerusalem is the center for three major religions; Jewish (75%), Muslim (20%), Christian and other faiths (5%). Four quarters made up the Old City: Jewish, Muslim, Christian, and Armenian. Each of these religions can be characterized by their attire. Muslim men wore turbans, or keffiyeh. Picture a red-and-white or black-and-white checked cloth worn on the head and secured by a piece of rope, and that is a keffiyeh. They sported this to protect their head from the sun. They wore white robes or business suits. Arab women wore a khimar, which was a veil that covered their head and chest. Their robes were black or a layering of rich-colored, silk scarves. I admired their fashion sense.

Jewish men had long beards; clothed in black garb, they could be identified by the strictly Orthodox black hats. Jewish women wore dresses and a snood, a cross between a scarf and a hood.

Christian clergy dressed in a white collar and black suit. The other faiths blended into a mix of people. Tourists stood out by their clothing: jeans, and tennis shoes.

Each faith appeared to be in a hurry to arrive at their place of worship. An aura of spirituality descended over the city. The city was alive with movement.

Jews headed to the Western Wailing Wall as today was their Sabbath. They wrote prayers on pieces of paper and stuffed them into the crannies of the wall. Jews obey the laws in the Torah, the word of God given to Moses in the Old Testament. They donned a tallit, a prayer shawl, while praying. The term "Wailing Wall" comes from the Jews who mourn the destruction of the Second Temple.

Muslims proceeded to a mosque. The most famous mosque in Israel is the Dome of the Rock in Jerusalem, which occupied a massive esplanade on the Temple Mount. Muslims abide by the laws of their holy book, the Koran. They believe in one God, named Allah. Muhammad, their prophet, received revelations from Allah.

Christians strode to churches. They follow the Bible as the word of God.

In the Old City, loudspeakers blared the Salat, a Muslim call to prayer, five times a day. Christians rang bells at noon and at six in the evening for the *Angelus* prayer. Various languages permeated the air.

It surprised me to observe that people co-exist, and to my untrained eye, get along in a country rife with a history of war. I felt safe, but the gathering of armed young men and women in military dress reminded me of the dangers that lurk on any day in Jerusalem. In contrast, I had no fears when I traveled in the U.S.

Aromas of various ethnic foods filtered through the atmosphere in the narrow streets of the Old City. We had a good breakfast before we left the hotel, but the new spices enticed my appetite. Maybe at lunch we could try a new entrée.

Our agenda for today was to walk the Via Dolorosa, the path through the Old City in Jerusalem that followed the last steps of Christ. For Christians, the path was sacred. Today it has become a commercial opportunity for vendors. They offered tourists an awkward cross to carry as they traced Jesus' steps. The cross was not heavy, but the meaning carried great weight. I carried the cross between the third and fourth station where Jesus fell the first time. The experience provoked me. We stopped at the fourteen stations and pondered on the relevance of each. Tears stung my eyes as I contemplated what Jesus did for my redemption. We sang the Lenten song lyric, *Were you there when they crucified, my Lord?* The encounter was so moving that it seemed odd that life could "go on as usual" for the other tourists, merchants opening their shops, and children playing in the streets.

When Jesus stumbled along the Via Dolorosa, he drew crowds of His followers. The crowd of believers lamented the undeserved sentence of this sinless man by crying and groaning as Jesus carried the cross. Criminals who committed serious crimes staggered this way to Calvary, the site of the crucifixion.

We ended the walk at the Church of the Holy Sepulchre. The church was in the center of the Old City. On entering the dimly lit church, we climbed the steep stone stairs to Golgotha (Calvary), where Christ died on the cross to redeem us. The stone of Golgotha was under an altar, so we had to kneel to touch it. This sent shivers down my body. I couldn't get my head around the experience I had after I touched the stone where Christ had died.

The Church of the Holy Sepulchre had the anointing stone, fifty feet from where they had crucified Christ. I considered Joseph of Arimathea and the women who anointed Christ before they buried Him. I envisioned their tender love for Christ and the sorrow they felt for this King of the Jews. Women rubbing Jesus' feet jogged a memory of when my mother was bedridden before her death. As I massaged her arthritic hands with lotion, it comforted both of us. That experience came to life as I contemplated on how the women cared for Jesus.

An aedicule, a tiny chapel inside the church, contained Christ's tomb in the Church of the Holy Sepulchre. We had to bend over to enter the tomb. Jesus died on the cross for us to live. When God the Father resurrected Christ, his Son's tomb became a sacred place. As I touched the marble slab over the tomb, my heart overflowed with gratitude for what Christ accomplished.

At Mass, Fr. Mike said, "Meditate on what Jesus has done for you. Persevere in your daily crosses and give Jesus your problems." Cancer was my cross. I needed to turn to God and ask for help to understand my disease.

After Mass, we sought a nearby food vendor and bought a falafel in a pita. It tasted delicious. I perused several tiny shops before we exited the Old City through the Jaffa Gate. A beggar approached us. Roni told us, "Great actor and best pick-pocket in Jerusalem."

We boarded the bus for the first time today and rode to Ein Kerem and the Church of the Annunciation. This village was where Mary had trekked to visit her cousin, Elizabeth, who was pregnant with John the Baptist. The ninety-mile landscape between Nazareth and Ein Kerem was hilly and rocky. It would have been a difficult journey for a young, pregnant Mary, and taken her ten days to make the trip on foot or by donkey. I don't think it was a journey I would have liked. Jeff Cavins encouraged us to ask Mary, the Queen Mother, to intercede for us. One of my favorite memories from Ein Kerem was a sculpture depicting these two holy, pregnant women meeting and displaying their tender devotion to each other.

We returned to the Olive Tree Hotel for dinner where we ate our evening meal with fellow pilgrims. After dinner, Jim and I went to our room to organize the treasure of gifts we had bought.

January 15, 2012

What to do on a free day in Jerusalem? Jim and I awakened at four-thirty in the morning to return with Fr. Mike Schmitz and other pilgrims to the Church of the Holy Sepulchre. We wore layers in the cool morning and walked under a starlit sky for the twenty-minute walk to the church. We were quiet, each of us thinking about what we had seen and what we would see again.

It was nice to go into the church without crowds. We clambered up the stone stairs to Golgotha, where the Jewish leaders, along with the Romans, had crucified Jesus. It was important for Jim and me to reflect on our faith through Jesus' accomplishment. *He* died for *our* salvation.

We revisited the main floor and touched the anointing stone. It was a large, marble rectangle on the floor with ornate candles hanging over it. From there, we returned to Christ's tomb, which accommodated two people. I wasn't teary, but grateful for Christ's obedience to his Father. My prayers were in thanksgiving to Christ. I reflected on how I would have reacted to Jesus' death if I had lived over two thousand years ago. Would I have been a follower? I wondered if He could teach me His ways.

Jim asked Fr. Mike to bless me again. I had never met Fr. Mike before this trip, yet he had a positive vibe that encircled him. Without drawing attention to himself, he stretched his hands over my head and asked the Lord to bless me. The blessing filled me with hope.

We strolled back to the hotel for breakfast at seven. Soon after, we departed for Mass at Notre Dame of Jerusalem Center. I appreciated the warmer weather and sunshine. This priest said, "Don't panic because you only have a few more days left in the Holy Land. In many ways, you need to be like the earth; take in the rain and let the surplus run off. You can take in the prayers, yet realize some of the prayers will soak in and other will run off. The scripture will be there when you need it. You are made for the glory of God, and He knows your name." My faith fulfilled me with my purpose on earth: to seek and know God.

After Mass, Jim and I opted to spend time in the Old City, entering through the Damascus Gate (meaning if you took that road, it led you to Damascus). Merchants crammed the narrow streets with colorful wares to draw tourists in to buy souvenirs. They hawked scarves, jewelry, pottery, purses, sandals, and trinkets. It took me back to my first visit to Chinatown in San Francisco, lots of importers and merchandise crammed into small spaces.

Jim thought he heard them plead, "Come in. Let me rip you off. At least I'm honest." Roni divulged a secret; barter with the shop owners. Bartering wasn't in my DNA, but I was happy to buy a few more gifts to bring home.

Children with curly dark hair frolicked under the canopied and constricted avenues. The air filled with laughter, music and chants. I heard many dialects, but couldn't name the languages.

The heavy scent of Middle Eastern spices, tobacco, and incense pervaded the atmosphere. The food we ate was flavorful with spices we had never tasted. Pita bread stuffed with vegetables and a Diet Coke satisfied us for lunch. Vibrant colors in clothing and in the displays of the merchants contributed to a rich essence to the city. Our three cameras filled up with photos. Jim photographed every church and site we visited.

Jim and I returned, once more, to the Church of the Holy Sepulchre. We discovered other sections of the poorly lit church. This was what we had come to see. Where Christ had fulfilled His ministry, but also to experience what He had achieved. After prayers for our loved ones, we hurried back to the hotel so I could take a nap before dinner. I didn't recognize how exhausting the outing had been.

January 16, 2012

We could go without coats today, choosing a long sleeve shirt and vest and dress slacks for the tour of the Jewish Quarter in the Old City. We entered through Zion Gate and made our way to the large, open plaza in front of the Western Wailing Wall. Jewish people, alongside large numbers of tourists, gathered here. I saw Jews praying and touching the wall. If you approached the wall, separated by a piece of rope, you had to go to the designated side for men or women.

People of any faith could write a prayer on a piece of paper, move forward to the wall, and insert the paper between the cracks. I scribbled a prayer for healing on a note card, folded it, approached the wall, and pushed it between the crevices. This simple act helped me connect with the Jewish people.

Monday was a common day for Bar Mitzvahs. We saw a procession for a thirteen-year-old boy, walking under a canopy, on his way to his Bar Mitzvah at the Wailing Wall. A drummer and a ram's horn player preceded the youth while friends and family danced in the streets. Since the Wailing Wall had sections for each gender, the mothers of those having a Bar Mitzvah had to stand on chairs to get a glimpse of their son's ceremony. I judged it rude to the mothers to be excluded from being at their son's side on such a special event, but that was their tradition.

In Jesus' time, the Temple was the heart of the political, economic, and religious ritual of ancient Israel. Jesus would have come to the Temple three times a year for the Holy Days in the Jewish calendar. I pictured the seventy-mile hike between Nazareth and Jerusalem. Jesus had been here! The reality that I walked where Jesus had walked washed over me with a sense of wonder.

As a youth, Jesus stayed behind in Jerusalem without his parents' knowledge. How frantic were Mary and Joseph as they sought their son? I would go crazy if I'd lost a child. Mary and Joseph found Jesus listening to the teachers. When Mary asked Jesus why He hadn't come with them, He replied, "I must be about my Father's business." Jesus was not afraid his parents had forgotten Him. Jesus left the teachers and obediently went home with his parents.

As an adult, Jesus taught in the Temple or on the southern steps of the Temple Mount. Jeff Cavins lectured here. "The stairs are arranged haphazardly, which signifies that you need to pay attention to the challenges in your life. In daily challenges, it is good to pray the Psalms. If you are hurt or betrayed, go to the Lord. Ask God what opportunity He wants me to take in my life. When I am weak, then I am strong."

I recognized how important it was to pay attention to the trials in life. My diagnosis had altered my life. In some ways it was a good alteration, because it forced me to slow down and gain a deeper appreciation for family, friends, and nature. I had more time for prayer and reflection. I needed to keep my focus on my faith.

Jim led the fourth Joyful mystery of the Rosary here, The Presentation in the Temple. He inspired me by our common beliefs.

Mass followed at the Church of St. Peter in Gallicantu, on top of Mt. Zion. Beautiful blue mosaics decorated the walls and ceilings. They built this church over the site of the High Priest Caiaphas' house, where Caiaphas held Jesus the night before His crucifixion. The church also commemorated where Peter denied Jesus three times before the cock crowed. The homily centered on Jesus and His thoughts the night before He died. I wondered, "Was He thinking of me?" Christ knew His role, along with mine, in the story of salvation history.

After Mass, we hopped on the bus for a short ride to the City of David. King David united Israel, and he built his palace and capital here, located south of the Temple Mount and the Old City of Jerusalem. The City of David offered a suitable view across the Kidron Valley to the Mount of Olives.

King Hezekiah built a tunnel under the City of David. It was a means to provide water to the city from the Springs of Gihon, located outside the walls of the city. We walked in one of three tunnels, the dry tunnel, to the Pool of Siloam. Jesus restored sight to a blind man here. Jesus told the blind man, "Go and wash at the Pool of Siloam." The blind man did as Jesus instructed and found he could see. Siloam means "sent" and Jesus was the Messiah "sent" from heaven. I was learning little fragments of Hebrew and attempted to assemble the puzzle of the words.

We returned to the hotel for our farewell feast. After the meal, it was customary to thank our bus drivers and guides. Pilgrims volunteered to toast and roast those that had provided expert interpretations for the places we had seen and the safety the bus drivers used on the narrow roads. One person sang, *If I Were a Rich Man*, from the show *Fiddler on the Roof*. We shared laughter and newfound friendships before we disappeared to finish packing.

January 17, 2012

We didn't have to be ready early today, so we lingered at breakfast on our last day in the Holy Land. After checking out of the hotel, the pilgrims boarded the buses that took us to another nature preserve, the Bet Guvrin Caves. At these caves, we saw the columbarium used for raising pigeons. They sacrificed pigeons in the temple at the time of Christ. Roni pointed out the carob tree, which contains nourishing seeds. He said, "In ancient times, a carob seed was used as a standard unit of measurement of weight. That is where the term, carat, originated for measuring diamonds."

The most astonishing set of caves were the bell caves. When the people of ancient Israel dug down about twenty-feet from the surface, they found chalk deposits. It was easy to haul out the soft chalk. The large, open caves that remained had wonderful geologic markings and great acoustics. Roni told us that his daughter had her prom there.

We continued to the Elah Valley where David slew Goliath. At this season of the year, the valley was green with a new crop of wheat. Jeff Cavins taught that this was the place between the two hills where the Jews and the Philistines had camped. "Remember in the battle zones of your life, you must ask God for help."

I was in awe that we were standing in the field where such a historic event had occurred. Jeff urged us to pick up a stone to take home to remind us that God wants to help us. I brought my stone home and put it on my kitchen windowsill where I could see it every day.

Rain canceled the picnic planned for this site, so we moved to a strip mall that included a McDonalds. Since we were in Israel, cheeseburgers and milkshakes were not on the menu due to kosher food rules. The McDonalds offered other familiar choices and combo meals. I ordered a simple hamburger, French fries, and a Diet Coke.

We celebrated our final Mass at the Church of St. Peter in the port city of Jaffa. The priest recapped, "You are leaving Israel with a happy heart after the new experiences and new friends." At the end of Mass, the priests anointed me and other sick pilgrims. I had told a few selected pilgrims about my diagnosis because I didn't want my cancer to define me. It was humbling to have the pilgrims pray for me and others in the group who were sick. After an eleven-day pilgrimage, I had admiration for my fellow pilgrims and their devotion to the faith. Some of the pilgrims could quote verses and text from the Bible. I could not. I was glad that no one had a game of Bible Trivial Pursuit because I wouldn't know the answers to win.

Jeff Cavins and his ministry offered me a greater awareness of the Bible. He shared his knowledge of Biblical history, the languages, geography, cultures and customs from long ago. I hoped to continue to grow in studying my faith.

We were eager to get to the airport at ten at night to clear security. Israel took safety seriously. Jim made the mistake of changing his shirt in a bathroom in the terminal before going through security. After that, security chose Jim "at random" at every security checkpoint. Later, we learned that everyone who comes into the terminal was under surveillance. Since he had changed his shirt, he was a marked man. Any activity that aroused suspicion called for extra security. Trained informants apparently posed as custodians.

I don't know if they consider a departure time of one in the morning as a "red eye," but we had a twelve-hour flight to New York. With layovers in New York and Minneapolis, we arrived in Rochester at six the next evening.

As I shared my experiences, individuals often asked me, "How do you know an event took place at this location?" Earthquakes and war destroyed buildings, and the next generation built over the ruins. History, geography, archeology, the Bible, and faith take these things into account when commemorating a Bible event. The people who venerate the event make it a holy place.

The memories of visiting biblical sites, noticing colors, tasting Middle East flavors, hearing many languages, witnessing traditions, and experiencing the culture, will live with me for the rest of my lifetime.

At home, the pilgrimage invaded my dreams. I meditated on the images and the lessons the Holy Land etched in my brain. I came home with a profound awareness of my connection to God.

My message is one of faith and hope and trust. Don't lose sight of God's gift to us: eternal life in heaven. Blessings to everyone that has traveled with me on my cancer journey!

APPENDIX

The February 2012 Health Report

I received good news from Dr. Buckner. "Your tumor has shrunk significantly. It might be several years or more before it reappears. Researchers have published a study that shows patients with an oligoastrocytoma with 1p19q markers have a *dramatic* response with chemotherapy."

I was lucky to have those chromosomal markers.

I will need MRIs and blood work every three months for the next three years to render there is no further growth in the tumor.

My "gift" of cancer is the fact I have learned with everything in life, I can trust God!

EPILOGUE

I have been symptom-free for four years now. I had been on a quarterly follow-up for two years, then I moved to semi-annual check-ups, and now I have moved to annual follow-ups with the doctors. There is something freeing when you don't have to think of blood draws and MRIs.

I will be on the medication, Keppra, for the rest of my life to control any seizures. The only bad thing about being on Keppra is that I cannot drink alcoholic beverages. That is a minor inconvenience in the grand scheme of life.

As I reflect on my cancer journey with an oligoastrocytoma, I know I was fortunate when family and friends offered prayers on my behalf. I continue to trust in God and follow the path he has created for me.

I have been blessed by two more grandchildren. Tim and Jane welcomed a son, Jamie. John and Lindsay had another daughter named Maren.

Jim retired in November 2014. He welcomes the opportunity to golf when the weather is good. I have returned to exercise classes at the Dan Abraham Healthy Living Center several times a week. Along with church involvement, it has taken me close to three years to write this memoir. I am always aware of God's beauty and His Divine plan.

In October 2015, Kathleen married Corey Fruin, the young man we had met at the Madison football game. They have made Rochester their home for now.

Never give up hope. Call on the Lord when you encounter struggles. He has a plan for you to reach heaven.

ABOUT THE AUTHOR

Mary McCarthy is a first-time author. In her book *A Pilgrimage of Hope: A Story of Faith and Medicine,* she addresses the medical and spiritual needs to overcome a diagnosis of brain cancer. She lives in Rochester, Minnesota, with her husband. She has three married children and five grandchildren.

CPSIA information can be obtained at www.ICGtesting.com
Printed in the USA
LVOW11s0313170915

454462LV00002B/2/P